JACQUES LACARRIERE
The Gnostics

Foreword by
LAWRENCE DURRELL

Translated from the French by
NINA ROOTES

CITY LIGHTS BOOKS
San Francisco

Cover by Rikki Ducornet

2nd Printing, 1991

Library of Congress Cataloging-in-Publication Data:
Lacarrière, Jacques. 1925-
   [Gnostiques. English]
   The Gnostics / by Jacques Lacarrière: translated from the French by Nina Rootes:
   with a forword by Lawrence Durrell.
   p. cm.
   Translation of: Les gnostiques.
   Reprint. Originally published : London : Owen, 1977.
   Bibliography: p.
   ISBN 0-87286-243-7 : $6.95
   1. Gnosticism. I. Title.
BT1390.L2713   1989   89-34170
273'. 1—dc20   CIP

City Lights Books are available to bookstores through our primary
distributor: Subterranean Company. P. O. Box 168, 265 S. 5th St.,
Monroe, OR 97456. 503-847-5274. Toll-free orders 800-274-7826.
FAX 503-847-6018. Our books are also available through library
jobbers and regional distributors. For personal orders and catalogs,
please write to City Lights Books, 261 Columbus Avenue, San
Francisco CA 94133.

CITY LIGHTS BOOKS are edited by Lawrence Ferlinghetti and
Nancy J. Peters and published at the City Lights Bookstore, 261
Columbus Avenue, San Francisco, CA 94133.

CONTENTS

FOREWORD

This is a strange and original essay — a sort of poetic meditation on the vanished Gnostics of Egypt whose total refusal to believe in the world as outlined by the Christian theologians led to their destruction both in Egypt and in Bosnia, and lastly at Montségur,* that Thermopylae of the Gnostic soul. I should stress that this is more a work of literature than of scholarship, though its documentation is impeccable. It is as convincing a reconstruction of the way the Gnostics lived and thought as D. H. Lawrence's intuitive re-creation of the vanished Etruscans.

The documentation we possess on the Gnostics is almost as scanty as that on the Etruscans and much of it comes from the opposition, so to speak, from the Church Fathers. Lacarrière has used his sources with skill and honesty and this essay is of a burning topicality to a world which is also playing at Gnosticism — the pathetic cockroach world of the anti-hero with his anti-memoirs, not to mention his anti-poetry. How noble in comparison with this shallow hippie defeatism is the grand poetic challenge of the Gnostics. They refused to countenance a world which was less than perfect, and they affronted the great lie of Lucifer-Mammon with the hopeless magnificence of the Spartan three hundred.

All that we need to know about the author is that he is a wanderer and a poet; he is neither a scholar nor a journalist. The Indians would call him a 'searcher' — and indeed he has spent a considerable time in both India and Egypt and has studied the languages and landscapes of both; in the latter country it is impossible not to be struck by the history of these obliterated sects which clustered around the central idea of Gnosticism and which were finally scattered to the four winds of heaven by the 'true Christians,' the anthropophagous elect of heaven in whose mental

* On 16 March, 1244 some two hundred Cathar heretics were burnt on a huge communal pyre after the capitulation of the fortress of Montségur.

7

universe we now live — on the gold-standard of brotherly love. Lacarrière has given us a Cuvier-like reconstruction of the great Gnostic refusal of the lie, and their refusal to share the world of that lie with its religious leaders. The courage of this despair is poetic in the highest degree and this splendid poem renders it full justice.

LAWRENCE DURRELL

INTRODUCTION

Eighteen centuries separate us from the Gnostics. Eighteen centuries during the course of which wars, persecutions and massacres, causing the deaths of thousands, have amply justified the total suspicion in which they held this world and the creatures that inhabit it. In everything that contemporary history sets before our eyes — the ever more blatant contempt for the individual man, the fallacy of ideologies, the wars or military interventions openly carried on for the profit of the combined interests of capitalism and socialism, the daily erosion of liberty and the fascination of violence — in all this, a Gnostic of today would see nothing more than the magnified image of the dramas which were familiar to him, and the inevitable outcome of that everlasting outrage, the very existence of the world and of humanity *as they are.*

Who then were these people, lucid enough to look at creation with eyes stripped of all consoling self-deceptions, sensitive enough to feel, in all its unbearable extremity, the anguish of an eternity forever promised and forever denied, sincere enough to accept in their own lives all the implications of this total rejection of the world, and to behave, everywhere and at all times, as unsubjugated outsiders?

The term Gnostic is vague, encompassing several distinctly different meanings. But, historically speaking, it acquired a particular meaning during the early centuries of our era. On the Eastern shores of the Mediterranean, in Syria, Samaria and Egypt, at the moment when Christianity was feeling its way, and when so many prophets and messiahs were travelling the high roads of the Orient, founding short-lived communities here and there, certain men called Gnostics, that is to say 'men who know,' were also setting up important communities, grouped around various masters and female initiates of a teaching that was radically different from all the others.

9

For the moment, I can do no more than sketch in the broad out-
lines of this complex, fascinating message, which will be drawn in
greater detail throughout the text of the book. Gnosis is knowledge.
And it is on knowledge — not on faith or belief — that the Gnostics
rely in order to construct their image of the universe and the in-
ferences they drew from it: a knowledge of the origin of things, of
the real nature of matter and flesh, of the destiny of a world to
which man belongs as ineluctably as does the matter from which
he is constituted. Now this knowledge, born out of their own meditations or from the secret teachings which they claim to have had
from Jesus or from mythical ancestors, leads them to see the whole
of material creation as the product of a god who is the enemy of
man. Viscerally, imperiously, irremissibly, the Gnostic feels life,
thought, human and planetary destiny to be a failed work, limited
and vitiated in its most fundamental structures. Everything, from
the distant stars to the nuclei of our body-cells, carries the materi-
ally demonstrable trace of an original imperfection which only
Gnosticism and the means it proposes can combat.

But this radical censure of all creation is accompanied by an
equally radical certainty which presupposes and upholds it: the
conviction that there exists in man something which escapes the
curse of this world, a fire, a spark, a light issuing from the true God
— that distant, inaccessible stranger to the perverse order of the
real universe; and that man's task is to regain his lost homeland by
wrenching himself free of the snares and illusions of the real, to
rediscover the original unity, to find again the kingdom of this
God who was unknown, or imperfectly known, to all preceding
religions.

These convictions were expressed through a radical teaching
which held almost all the systems and religions of former times to
be null and void. In spite of its links with some philosophies of the
time, and apart from minor reservations — since they borrowed
certain beliefs indiscriminately from various systems, prophets or
sacred books — one can say that Gnosticism is a profoundly
original thought, a *mutant thought.*

This rejection of all systems, and of a world governed not by
men but by shadows or semblances of men — whom I will call
pseudanthropes — forced them to live on the fringes of all estab-

lished society, and to preach a refusal to compromise with false institutions, a refusal to procreate, to marry, to live in families, or to obey temporal powers, whether pagan or Christian.

To sum up the essential position of the Gnostics in still simpler terms, let us say that in their eyes the evil which taints the whole of creation and alienates man in body, mind, and soul, deprives him of the awareness necessary for his own salvation. Man, the shadow of man, possesses only a shadow of consciousness. And it is to this one task that the Gnostics of the first centuries AD deliberately devoted themselves, choosing paths which were not only unorthodox but which, moreover, greatly scandalized their contemporaries: to create in man a true consciousness, which would permit him to impart to his thoughts and deeds the permanence and the rigour necessary to cast off the shackles of this world.

Let us, then, open the first dossier on this monumental undertaking, launched against the entire universe, against the immensity of the firmament, against man's original alienation and the falsity of systems and institutions, and let us begin at the beginning . . . with the sky.

The Workings of the World

> The death of a bee, assassinated by his queen, is charged with as much meaning as the massacres of Dachau.
>
> R. ABELLIO
> *Les yeux d'Ezéchiel sont ouverts*

I

THE PERFORATED VEIL

When all the complicated calculations
prove false, when the philosophers
themselves have nothing more to tell
us, we may be forgiven for turning to
the meaningless twitter of the birds or
to the distant counterweight of the
stars.

MARGUERITE YOURCENAR
Memoirs of Hadrian

What emotions does the sight of the sky inspire in us, if not praise, enthusiasm, and admiration? It is vast, infinite, immutable, omnipresent; it eludes the relative and the measurable; it is a parameter of the incommensurable. But in this concert, which we consider natural and which celebrates dawn, zenith, nadir, and twilight with equal assurance, discordant notes sometimes jar the ear. To be vast is good. To be infinite is too much. To possess planets and stars is an incontestable triumph. But to possess them by the million, to teem with stars which are so many eyes trained upon the world each night as if tracking our dreams, is to wield excessive power, to display a very suspect splendour. Something in this immensity turns and meshes its gears with a regularity so precise as to be disquieting; and exactly for whom—or against whom—this mechanism deploys its flaming wheelworks, we do not know.

So, in this simple look directed at the celestial vault, the Gnostics find themselves confronted with the ultimate nature of reality: what is this matter which is by turns full and empty, dense and tenuous, luminous and dark, of which our sky is made? Is this dark shore, this tenebrous tissue, this interstitial shadow wherein the stars seem pricked like incandescent pores, constituted of matter or of space? Is the 'real' sky nothing but its light, these winking eyes

on the ocean of night, or is it at one and the same time that which
shines and that which does not, a fire flaming and dark by turns?
Do its shores and its black abysses comprise a nothingness, an
absence of light, or are they the concrete material which inter-
poses itself between our earth and the distant fires which it
obscures?

No doubt this question will seem absurd, or at least premature,
in the age of the Gnostics. Nevertheless, it is implicit at the very
starting-point of their thought. Since man, in their view, is a fragment of the universe, and since the body of the one and the space
of the other proceed from a simple material, both must obey the
same laws. Man is a mirror in which one can discover the reduced
and condensed image of the sky, a living universe carrying within
him, in his body and in his psyche, fires and dark shores, zones of
shadow and of light. Are these lights and shadows simply forms
split off from a single material, or two materials of opposing
nature? All our existence, all our choices as thinking hominids are
vitally implicated in this simple question. Thus, the Gnostics
searched the splendours and the terrors of the sky to find an answer
to our own duality. Never was there asked a more pertinent
question and never were the stars scanned so earnestly.

And it seems that what struck these men most forcibly, as they
watched throughout the Egyptian nights, is the dark portion of the
sky — the vastness, the omnipresence, the heavy opacity of that
blackness. It hangs over us like a veil, a wall of shadow encircling
the earth, a tenebrous dome through which appear, here and there,
through chinks, faults and gaps, the glittering fires of another
world. A gigantic black lid seals in our universe and encompasses us
with its opacity.

Dark wall, black lid, circle of shadow. And beyond that, in a second
circle, the fire of the planets, the stars and all the heavenly bodies.
The eye apprehends this other world by means of the luminous dots
cut out of the fabric of the darkness in the shape of constellations,
the sparkling lace perforating the tissue of the cosmic night. Why
did the being — the god or demiurge — who thus perforated the
veil of our sky, trace these enigmatic stencilled patterns that echo

the familiar shapes of our world? Because, without a doubt, they are the sign of something, the sketch for some plan; they are messages or symbols scattered across the celestial vault. For example, one Gnostic sect, the Peratae (an obscure name meaning Those Who Pass Through), discovered in the constellation of the Serpent or the Dragon the very meaning of the genesis of the cosmos. It is a curious constellation, one of the most vast in the boreal sky, yet one to which little attention is paid. It stretches its sinuous shapes between Ursa Major and Ursa Minor, its tail lost in the direction of Gemini, its triangular head pointed towards the pole star. Its outline lacks the geometric precision of the Bear, the elegance of the Swan (Cygnus), or the severity of the Scorpion (Scorpio). But coiled as it is round the northern pole, as if suckling on the navel of the sky, one can understand why it should quickly become charged with symbolic importance.

The Peratae, who specifically regarded the Serpent as the first Gnostic in the world, the one who possessed primordial knowledge and had tried to communicate it to the first man, in Eden, recognized in this constellation the symbol of the primordial Serpent and his implication in human destiny: 'If a person has eyes that know how to see, he will look upward to the heavens and he will see the beautiful image of the Serpent coiled there, at the place where the great sky begins. Then he will understand that no being in heaven or on earth or in hell was formed without the Serpent.'

And so, these constellations relate the earliest segment of the world's history and are distinct signs, well worth deciphering since each has its terrestial counterpart. Up there, the great Serpent, coiled around the roots of heaven. On earth, the Serpent of Eden, coiled around the roots of the Tree of Knowledge. The sky — like the Biblical myths which the Gnostics often interpreted in the manner of modern mythologists, seeking to read the hidden meaning (today we would say 'unconscious meaning') that underlies their images, symbols and analogies — the sky, then, is the first source of knowledge.

If one wished to apply a contemporary idiom to Gnostic cosmology, one could say that the first circle (the circle of shadow) represents the strictly solar system, and the second (the fire of the planets) the galactic system to which we belong. But beyond the second circle the Gnostics imagined others — varying in number — right up to the ultimate centre which constitutes the source and the root of the entire universe. These intermediary worlds, these circles ranged in echelons up to the navel of the world, are totally invisible to us. It is through intuition, or rather through revelation, through gnosis, that the Gnostic knows of their existence. For, judging by all the evidence, the Gnostics built a pure mental construction — rather strange and refreshing, like the systems of the physicians of the Ionian school in Greece — upon an *a priori* vision of the universe.

One could say that these other worlds, presaged and divined by Gnostic speculation, in fact represent what modern astronomy calls nebulae, spirals, and extra-galactic clusters. A Gnostic like Basilides calls this world beyond the second circle, beyond the plants and the sphere of fixed stars, 'the hyper-cosmic world'. Therein resides the Supreme Being, the God-Nothingness, guardian of all destiny, all becoming, retainer of all seeds, powers, and potentialities; the purely intelligible fire which held, and still holds, the seeds of every-thing that fell thereafter into the inferior circles (supralunar and sublunar), and became animate and inanimate matter, forms, in-carnations, stones, trees, and flesh. It can be seen that the distances that separate all these worlds from each other are measured in terms of weight. Just as the semen of man, the minute, invisible seed possessing a scarcely measurable weight, acquires size and weight as it develops, so do the primordial seeds, the potentialities of a hyper-cosmic world, acquire weight by falling into the lower world, becoming more and more dense in substance.

It seems, then, that for the Gnostics there exist several states of matter: an igneous, superior state which belongs to the hyper-world, and successive states corresponding to the different circles, graded as the seeds materialize and take on darkness, opacity, gravity. Our own matter, that of the earth, plants, and all living creatures, is in some way the seed of the ethereal particles of the hyper-world, but grown infinitely heavier. Little by little, these particles have fallen down to our level as the result of a primordial drama which comprises the history of our universe, in the same manner that particles of dust and débris are slowly deposited at the bottom of marine abysses to form sediment. All the beings of our world are, in the eyes of the Gnostics, the sediment of a lost heaven.

And from the bottom of this dark sea, man perceives nothing of the luminous surface of the upper world except in ephemeral forms, fleeting reflections, evanescent phantoms which are like those phosphorescent fish that alone illuminate the age-old darkness of the great ocean depths. And our matter, because it is heavy, because it is dark — the darkest and heaviest of all — is also the least dynamic, the most immobile, as fixed and as heavy as atoms reduced to their nuclei. Immobility, the glacial cold of matter and flesh deprived of primal fire and sinking ineluctably towards that absolute zero which is the final stage of material death.

The implications of this image of creation, split into several universes of which the last — ours — is totally separated from the others by a barrier of dense shadow, are obviously profound. Weight, cold, and immobility are at once our condition, our destiny, and our death. To surrender oneself to weight, to increase it in all senses of the term (by absorbing food, or by procreating, weighing the world down with successive births), is to collaborate in this unhappy destiny, to ratify the primordial fall which is the cause of it, to ally oneself with the work of death undertaken by the being or beings who provoked this tragic cleavage. In modern terms, it is hastening the trend towards what we call entropy. Curiously enough, the Gnostics perceived, albeit summarily and imperfectly, the fact that the destiny of the material world tends towards inertia. The task of the Gnostic, therefore, is to climb this fatal slope, in the literal and in the figurative sense, to try to cross the dividing wall, to regain, by a progressive shedding of the alienating weight of his body and his psyche, the higher world from which we should never have fallen. To discard or lighten all the matter of this world, that is the strange end the Gnostics pursued.

I will say but little for the moment of the reasons for this initial split, this radical separation between the worlds, which condemns us to live in the darkest circle, this fall which makes man the prisoner of alienating matter. I will simply state that, at a certain moment in the dawn of time, when seeds were in their earliest awakening and all possibilities virgin, one of the inhabitants of the hyper-world — god, demiurge, angel or aeon (a term which appears frequently in Gnostic cosmology and which signifies an *immortal,* a living and personalized being) — one of these creatures, through error, pride, or fecklessness, intervened in the unfolding of the world and provoked disturbances, vibrations, and fibrillations of igneous matter which brought about its progressive degradation and its descent towards the lower circles. The world in which we live is not only opaque, heavy, and given over to death, but is above all a world born of a monumental machination; a world that was not foreseen, not desired, flawed in all its parts; a world in which every thing, every being, is the result of a cosmic misunderstanding. In this whirlpool of errors, this universal shipwreck which is the history of matter and of man, we on earth are rather like survivors condemned to eternal solitude, planetary detainees who are the victims of injustice on a truly cosmic scale. Stars, ether, aeons, planets, earth, life, flesh, inanimate matter, psyche — all are implicated, dragged into this universal disgrace.

Fortunately, the gaps, the perforations which shine in the celestial wall of our prison show that a possible way of escape exists. In the star-studded night, the Gnostic knows that not all contact with the higher circles is irremediably lost, and that perhaps he can conquer his fate, break the ancient curse which made the world a cheat and a sham, and cast us down, far from the sparkle and the blazing illumination of the hyper-world, down to the gloomy circle in which we live, this 'circle of dark fire.'

II

THE DARK FIRE

Injustice governs the universe. All that
is made and all that is unmade therein
carries the imprint of a corrupt frag-
ility, as if matter were the fruit of an
outrage in the womb of nothingness.

EMILE CIORAN
A Short History of Decay

To know our true condition, to realize that we are condemned to
live under a fantastic mass of darkness, beneath oceans and successive circles; to know that man, atrophied and infirm, vegetates in
submarine lairs like the proteus, that blind eel-like creature that
lives in subterranean waters, naked and white (or rather albino,
since white is still a colour, after all) . . . to know this is the first step
in Gnostic thought.

The same piercing look that the Gnostics cast upward to the sky
was also turned upon the earth. The earth of Egypt, burned by
solar fire, made up of deserts and arid mountains, or, around the
Nile, alluvial marshes which harbour a teeming life among a riot
of weeds and wild grasses, gave rise, perhaps, to the images they
formed of our planet. For this particular earth is moulded out of
violent contrasts, implacable struggles between the blinding light
of the days and the icy darkness of the nights, as if the elements
themselves, throughout the cycles of time, were powerless to do
anything but meet in headlong collision.

I remember walking on the outskirts of Alexandria one evening;
it was early autumn. The stars were shining with a fantastic clarity.
A swirling vapour rose from the ground to mingle with the
ambergris-like perfume of the marshes. The crystalline sky, so pure
that not a star winked, and the scalding earth, from which life itself

21

seemed to well up and overflow, offered two irreconcilable faces of reality: the mineral austerity of the infinite sky and the confused turbulence compounded of the sweat of the soil, this quivering veil of odours and the stench of putrefying matter.

But the truth is that neither the sky nor the earth, nor its odours, nor even — beyond these primary factors — the confusion of history and the disarray of systems in the age in which the Gnostics lived, can entirely explain this inquisitorial stare brought to bear upon our world. One feels that their vision of man and of the earth was dictated by a global feeling regarding matter itself, a feeling made up of both repulsion and fascination. Not that they were insensible to the beauty of the world or of the sky. A young Alexandrian Gnostic, Epiphanes, who died at the age of seventeen, wrote one of the most arresting pieces imaginable about the earth, the sun, justice and love. But what haunts the Gnostics above all else, when confronted by matter — by its opacity, its density, its compactness, its weight (and they felt this weight, this materiality, in those states that seem most subtle: the trembling of water, the wind of the desert, the shimmering of the stars) — what haunts them is the intolerable awareness that this inhibiting matter is the result of an error, a deviation in cosmic order; that it is nothing but a poor imitation or a caricature of the original matter of the hyperworld. The heaviness, the sluggishness imparted to everything — from the air to a stone, from an insect to a man — is an unbearable constraint, an intolerable curse. And its consequences are multiple. For, added to the weight of matter and of living bodies, there is the inevitable heaviness of the spirit. Our thinking is bound by the same constraints as are our bodies; it collides against the same barriers and is dragged down by the weight of the same contingencies. The majority of Gnostics expressed this dullness of the spirit — inherent in the matter of which we are composed — by a simple and revealing analogy: that of sleep. Sleep is to consciousness what weight is to the body: a state of death, inertia, a petrification of the psychic forces. We sleep. We spend our lives asleep. And only those who are aware of it can hope to break down these walls of mental inertia, to awaken in themselves the spark which, in spite of all, still glows within us, like a tear in the veil of corporeal night.

To awaken, to be alert, to keep vigil, these are the recurring themes in Gnostic texts. If Hermes is one of the favourite gods in their pantheon, it is because he is the personification of *The Wide-Awake,* the god to whom Homer long ago attributed the power to 'awaken, with his golden wand, the eyes of those who sleep.' Since Hermes was also the god who acted as what is pompously called a 'psychopomp' in ancient mythology (that is to say, one who accompanies souls through the kingdom of the dead, guiding them to the tribunal of the three infernal judges), he became known as the one who keeps his eyes wide open, like a living being, even in the realm of shadows, and who stays awake in the very heart of death. In any case, the names and attributes of those whom the Gnostics elevated to the rank of Initiates do not matter. What does matter is to perceive, over and above the meanderings of mythological or of theoretical systems, the existence and the quest for an asceticism and a specific power: the ability to keep one's eyes open, to refuse sleep, to awaken to a true consciousness of oneself.

If the Gnostics thus held sleep to be the most baneful condition of life, it was not only because it has the appearance of death, but because it also implies a return to immobility, a surrender to the tentacular inertia of the world. In the Greek myth of Endymion, this young and lovely shepherd lay down to sleep one night and was discovered by Selene, the Moon, who fell so violently in love with him that she begged Zeus never to let him awaken. She wanted Endymion to keep his eternal youth, but at the price of eternal sleep — and this same Endymion, prematurely embalmed, still living, was for the Gnostics an image of our condition and the proof of the obvious perversion of the gods, or the false gods, responsible for our world. To condemn a young and beautiful creature never to wake again, on pain of instant death, is not this the very apogee of sadism, something only a god could conceive? This, then, is the fate to which the frightful demiurge, the ignoble aeon who perverted the world's history, has condemned us from the very beginning of time (which he must have called into being together with weight, for the Gnostics see time as a condition appropriate to damned matter): to sleep our whole lives away without even knowing it, and without — like Endymion — being thereby saved from death.

To put it in other terms, our world, the circle of dark fire, is the domain of evil. This term is to be understood not in the moral but in the biological sense. The evil lies in the existence of matter itself, in so far as it is a parody of creation, a fraudulent arrangement of the first seeds; it lies in the existence of this sleep of the soul which has beguiled us into taking as reality that which is nothing but the illusory world of dreams; these are all the given data — today we would say all the structures — of our daily universe. Our world exudes evil from every pore, and our thinking being is tied to evil as ineluctably as our physical being is tied to the carbon in our body-cells. At this level, certainly, a kind of vertigo seizes us as we catalogue the ramifications of this cancer that pervades all the horrors of the contingent world. We bathe in evil as if in the bosom of a polluted sea, and the waters of the soul are powerless to wash us clean, unless we use the methods recommended by the Gnostics. Hence the fundamentally corrupt character of all human enterprises and institutions: time, history, powers, states, religions, races, nations — all these ideas, all these systems which man has invented, are tainted with this primary flaw.

In spite of what many historians of Gnosticism may have said, I believe that certain Gnostics reached these somewhat discouraging conclusions not so much out of pig-headedness as out of rational observation of the natural world and human behaviour. The smallest fact prompted them to think that evil forces are constantly being unleashed upon our heads. Thus, the simplest phenomenon, and the most elemental to boot — that of nutrition — would have been for the Gnostics a typical example of this maleficent inter-action, for the very act of nourishing oneself, of sustaining life, specifically implies the death of other living species. Each birth, each perpetuation of life, increases the domain of death. It is a never-ending circle, as vertiginous as the whirlpool of the stars or the cycle of time.

In this unending circle, the simple fact of living, of breathing, feeding, sleeping and waking, implies the existence and the growth of evil. What Darwinians were later to call natural selection and the survival of the fittest had already been observed by Gnostics and was in their eyes a flagrant proof of the fundamental depravity of the universe. But this inherent vice, which the Hebrews and

Christians saw as the stamp of original sin, and therefore wholly the responsibility of man, appeared to the Gnostics, on the contrary, as a statute imposed on man. Man has absolutely nothing to do with the curse that is laid upon him: the one who is truly responsible is the sadistic and perverse demiurge who dared to dream up such a cruel world in all its minute detail.

For, in the last analysis, if this world were the work of a good and just God — and not that of an incompetent and profoundly malevolent demiurge — one would have to impute to that God the most infamous thoughts and imaginings, the most ruthless acts of repression. For how could a supreme God have conceived the incredible sequences, mechanisms, massacres, and annihilations that constitute the very practice of life itself? What warped mind could have invented the procreative act of the praying mantis, in which the female decapitates and then devours the male? What immeasurably sadistic being could have thought up the paralysing sting of the ammophilous wasp, which it sticks into the flesh of caterpillars, that they may be devoured alive by the larvae of the winged insect? Who dared to fashion the hideous sex — the cloaca — of the tortoise, apparently with the sole aim of throwing a spanner into the works of copulation? What paranoiac demiurge had the idea of creating *bonellia,* those marine worms whose male is only one-hundredth part the size of the female and lives in the oesophagus of his partner, if one can call the monster on whom he is an unwitting parasite a 'partner'?

Who determined, planned, established all these aberrant processes, these by-roads, these multiple bifurcations of life? Of course, at this point I am quite deliberately expressing myself in contemporary terms. The Gnostics were no doubt ignorant of the habits of ammophiles, praying mantises and *bonellia.* But the natural world of their own time provided other examples, not so subtle, but just as conclusive as evidence of the universal offence. The very existence of sex can only be the invention of a being who is himself obsessed, and it is no mere chance that several psychoanalysts have discovered that Gnostic attitudes, in so far as creation and procreation are concerned, are astonishingly similar to their own views.

Later, we shall take up in detail this inventory of the ramifications of evil, of the planetary cancer which gnaws even at our sky, which impregnates our cells and insinuates itself into our least thoughts, and we shall do so in the company of the Gnostics themselves. For the moment, let us take it as an accepted fact that the circle of dark fire to which our earth is subject is, above all, the domain of evil, a subtle, molecular evil that falls from the stars like the dew at night, to cover and cancel out even our ways of thinking.

Given this fact, that the Gnostic found himself living in a world eroded by this celestial rust, and literally locked out of the kingdom of light by cosmic bars and bolts; how, then, could he feel that his condition was anything but that of a prisoner deported to a doomed planet, an exile, a stranger lost in the heart of a hostile world?

III

THE STRANGER

But the great black anti-suns, wells of
truth in the essential conspiracy, in the
grey veil of the hump-backed sky,
come and go and suck one another in,
and men call them ABSENCES.

RENE DAUMAL

Today when we read the catalogue of the various forms of human
exploitation and alienation, as presented in the most politically
committed publications, one fact immediately becomes apparent:
such are the limitations of ideology (the new mythology of our age)
that this necessary denunciation, this indispensable catalogue of
human injustice is solely concerned with its social and political
aspects. In spite of what half a century of socialist experimentation
has shown us, we persist in believing that a change limited exclusively to the politico-economic domain and to the means of production can resolve the problems that confront us.

It seems a simple, obvious, and irrefutable fact that today, as in
the time of the Gnostics, the alienation of man is global; it is also
true that the economic, social, and political causes of alienation
should be removed first. But far from ending there, the problem
begins precisely at the moment when this first hurdle has been
cleared. If I try to imagine people like Basilides, Valentinus or
Carpocrates (Gnostics of whom we shall speak in detail later) living
today, I see them as either totally detached from all political con-
siderations, or, on the contrary, totally involved in the revolutionary struggle of our times (these two postures being, for these men,
two identical forms of the same asceticism). I see them on the
streets, handing out pamphlets signed *The Proletariat of the Stars,*
but also taking the struggle further, to limits almost inconceivable

27

nowadays (since for them a truly revolutionary combat could be
nothing less than total), waging war against the very nature of our
presence here on earth. Modifying the means of production, trans-
forming the nature of economic exchanges and the distribution of
wealth, *without tying these changes in with an asceticism operating
conjointly on man's mental structures,* could achieve nothing more
in their eyes than changing one master for another, and therefore
one alienating factor for another, all the more dangerous in that
people would believe they had abolished the causes of alienation.

The Gnostics were no less aware of social injustices than other
people, and I am convinced that they fully recognized how infuria-
ting their stance must have been to a mind sensitive to the material
miseries of the world. But, despite their detachment from society,
they were, after all, the only ones who had any inkling of the political implications of their position. For what were the Christians
doing during these centuries? As soon as the Church was accepted
and recognized, and the Roman Empire itself had become Christian, they began to wield their power through repressive measures
(they who had once been martyred themselves now made martyrs
of their old enemies), thus giving still further credence to the Gnostic contention that all power — whatever kind it might be — is a
source of alienation. Moreover, the Christians were to 'capitalize'
— to use our contemporary jargon — on the ferment of revolt
against human misery, by persuading the poor and the exploited
that they would take first place in heaven, so that from the perspective of Christian eschatology heaven appears to be a sort of
azure field in which there will be an almost unimaginable settling
of accounts, beside which the prophetic images of the Apocalypse
are but pale shadows.

The Christians, with their mythology of punishment and
reward, have totally evaded the daily problems of their times, and,
right down to our own age, have perpetuated acceptance of social
injustices and submission to established authority (with good
reason, since this authority was vested in them). The Gnostics, however, never ceased to preach opposition to the powers-that-be,
whether Christian or pagan, since for them there was no difference
between the two. Christianity postponed the solution of immediate
problems *sine die* — and here the expression is particularly apt,

as it conforms to eschatological hopes of abolishing time. The Gnostics, on the contrary, were the only ones to adopt a logical attitude — a radical and onerous one, but nevertheless consistent with their deepest feeling: the conviction that as thinking hominids they were totally alienated creatures, right down to their very encephalic cells, and condemned to lifelong enslavement, from which only a full awareness of man's inert and slumbering condition could save them.

So, to have done with this problem and give an exact definition of Gnostic thought — as I understand it, at least — all institutions, laws, religions, churches and powers are nothing but a sham and a trap, the perpetuation of an age-old deception.

Let us sum up: we are exploited on a cosmic scale, we are the proletariat of the demiurge-executioner, slaves exiled into a world that is viscerally subjected to violence; we are the dregs and sediment of a lost heaven, strangers on our own planet.

To be a stranger is, in its basic meaning, to appear as strange to others. I am not making puns here, for it is the innate strangeness of man which led the Gnostics to reflect on his origin, and on his terrestrial status. They used this term to express the disparity between the nature of the true man of the hyper-world and the abortive creature, the imitation man, that the demiurge managed to fashion and throw down into this circle of dark fire. The stranger's condition is inherently false. One cannot be a stranger except in relation to a non-stranger. Now in ancient times, he who was the opposite of a stranger — in political, civic and human terms—was the autochthon. The autochthon is the Athenian born in Athens, the Alexandrian born in Alexandria, in short, the citizen, but he is more than that: he is the man born of the very soil, bound to his native land by unbreakable biological bonds. Every stranger is, in some sense, the autochthon of another land. The fundamental difference that separates the Gnostics from their contemporaries is that, for them, their native 'soil' is not the earth, but that lost heaven which they keep vividly alive in their memories: they are the autochthons of another world. Hence their feeling of having fallen onto our earth like inhabitants from a distant planet, of having strayed into the wrong galaxy, and their longing to regain their true cosmic homeland, the luminous hyper-world that shimmers beyond the great nocturnal barrier. Their uprooting is not merely geographical but planetary. And to treat them as aliens in the political or civic sense — which is what happened — could be nothing but an absurd misunderstanding, like giving a Martian a temporary residence visa. For the Gnostics, all men were in the same condition, although they were the only ones who knew it, and the human community as a whole is implicated in this universal exile, this galactic diversion that has caused us to be dumped on the mud of planet earth.

The Gnostics must have felt this exile even more acutely in that they themselves constituted marginal communities, strangers or 'foreigners' in the narrow sense of the term, in the heart of a whole humanity of foreigners. The idea of calling oneself Egyptian, Greek, Roman or Syrian must have seemed ridiculous to them. Moreover, it is no mere chance that the Gnostic communities developed in the only cities of that period which were cosmopolitan in character: Alexandria, Antioch and Rome. One cannot imagine Gnostics in Gaul or Germania. Their own alien condition could freely nourish itself in these towns where the most diverse ethnic groups intermingled, and where the most essential transformations of the Mediterranean world took place between the first and the fourth centuries AD. Here there was an historical humus which justified the Gnostic feeling of exile, of being a planetary foreigner: 'I am *in* the world but not *of* the world' is the most basic Gnostic formula. It summarizes perfectly the feeling of being relegated to the lower depths of the cosmos, of living on a planet, and in a fleshly body, made of molecules that have agglomerated in the most dubious combinations, in complex and inextricable amalgams which, in some fashion, constitute the material support of our spiritual reclusion. The sadistic and perverse demiurge responsible for this world and our existence in it must have racked his brains to find these incredible combinations of molecules, these indissoluble aggregates of matter, which make any escape from the carnal and planetary prison impossible or, at the least, very aleatory. So the problem is simple, and one begins to understand how the Gnostics saw it: man, then, is a lifelong exile on a planet which is a prison for all mankind; he lives in a body which is a prison for the soul; he is the autochthon of a lost and invisible world.

These images or definitions seem to be constant repetitions. In the texts describing man's condition, the Gnostics repeat themselves endlessly, as if here again they are battering at the walls of a prison of words. The terms they use to describe the world here below resolve themselves into a few formulae which reappear over and over again: a 'hermetically sealed fortress,' 'prison,' 'cloaca,' 'slough,' 'desert.' It is the same for the human body: it is a 'tomb,' a 'gross garment,' a 'chain,' a 'trespasser,' a 'suffocating sea,' a 'vampire.' The point is that the history of man reproduces very closely the initial drama — and the farce — of the cosmos. Man, like the universe, is a failed creation, a lamentable imitation, the mere semblance of a man, a counterfeit man, or, in anthropological terms, a pseudanthrope. In man, the forgery is more immediately apparent than it is in the universe, for the human body is better known, and more accessible to us, than the light of the distant stars. Let us therefore summarize, as simply as possible, the precise reason for our being what we are, that is to say, trespassers in a body which is ill-suited to us.

In the beginning, in the world of possibilities and virtualities, an image of man was born in the intelligible brain of the true God of the highest circle: a potential man, the mental matrix of he whom the true God might one day have made real. This image was perceived by the demiurges, the archons or angels of the lower circles. How? Why? A mystery. But perceive it they did and were dazzled, as if by the light, the force, the beauty, the coherence which emanated from this mentally conceived Anthropos. They therefore decided to imitate and reproduce him.

Saturninus, a Gnostic who was teaching at Antioch in the reign of Hadrian, seems to have had some insight into this crucial instant of the celestial prehistory of our race. He reports that the angel-demiurges, confronted with this fascinating vision, cried out at once: 'Let us make a man in the semblance of this image.' They set to work, took clay and fashioned a man. But can one call the lamentable creature that took on life under their hands a man — this naked being, hominoid in appearance but incapable of standing upright on his atrophied legs, who 'lay on the ground, wriggling

like a worm'? Today, it must be admitted, this image has lost some
of the outrageous character it must have had in early times for those
who were not Gnostics, those who were steeped in the serenity of
Biblical images. For, presented like this, writhing clumsily in the
matrical mud, 'in the black waters,' this man, or this pre-man, had
all the characteristics of some amphibious beast. Anyone who has
seen reconstructions of the first amphibians to leave the domain of
water and reach dry land, anyone who has seen an Ichthyostega, a
Seymouria or an Ophiacodon, those creatures of the Mesozoic era
who foreshadowed terrestial reptiles, will realize that this pre-man
must, indeed, have resembled them. This creature, wailing discon-
certingly from a mouth still slimed with matrical clay, with its limbs
sketched in but incapable of supporting its body, bore only a remote
resemblance to the luminous and numinous image which had
called it into being. But the true God, seeing this error, this horror
crawling on the face of the earth and threatening to populate it,
took pity on the ineptitude of the angels. Into this wailing worm,
he breathed the spark of life, which instantly permitted him to
stand up and speak. *Homo bipedus* and *loquens* was born. And
thus our dual nature is explained: we are somewhat like a rectified
worm, an ex-amphibian set to rights by the indulgence of the true
God and endowed with a spark, a luminous fragment of the supreme Power.

At this stage of Gnostic anthropology, the consequent moral goes
right back to the source, so to speak. That which weighs us down,
makes us heavy, and sends us to sleep, is this cloacal matrix, this
borborian matter from which we were extracted; above all, it is
this basic flaw in our very structures that renders us incapable of
assuming our predestined mission—we have been odiously side-
tracked through the interference of sorcerers' apprentices. Only by
kindling the spark of life that lives in our corrupt flesh, and fanning
it into a blaze by means of a fitting asceticism, can we lighten the
heavy yoke of our bodies.

But it seems that one will never come to an end of all the logical
conclusions to be drawn from the simple fact of having been
fashioned from clay. For clay is by nature impermeable to water,
and indeed to air, and the human psyche—which comes from clay
just as the body does, though one could say it is more refined—is

also impermeable, or only very slightly permeable, to the light from above. Like those porcelain filters used for straining viruses, our psyches, in the finest instances, filter out certain particles of luminous matter from the heavenly heights, but man needs a great deal of concentration, vigilance, and ascetic practice to gather up this primordial light and isolate it from the stellar mud. Now, on the basis of these extrapolations (which, obviously, never figure in Gnostic texts in this form), let us hazard a more exact definition of man: a rectified worm, endowed with a divine spark which makes of him a biped *sapiens* and *loquens,* and with a psyche, a tenuous filter which strains out the splendours of the upper heavens. It is man's aim to collect these splendours, augment them, concentrate them within himself and thus acquire a sort of counter-weight to overcome the body's inertia and regain the salvatory firmament which the wall of darkness conceals from our sight.

And it is specifically through this struggle against the body's inertia and the soul's slumber, by practising techniques of physical and mental awakening, by a sort of 'long, immense and rational disordering of all the senses'—in short, by living a counter-life—that we may triumph over the material and spiritual order of this world.

IV

THE BODY'S BASTARD BIRTH

Into your womb I come to accomplish the rite
The rhythmic return to the prenatal country
The animal symbol of ages-old rapture
Into your womb I come to lay my offering
Of balm and venom
Blind and annihilated in the grottoes of being . . .

ROGER-GILBERT LECOMTE
Sacre et massacre de l'amour

Five fingers. Four limbs. Two eyes. A brain. And a name, too: *homo bipedus, sapiens, loquens.* It is easy to describe man with the detachment of an inhabitant of Sirius. But the Gnostics *did* have this feeling that they came from Sirius, or rather from a world that was even farther away, stranger and still more puzzling, a world beyond Sirius. Perhaps this explains the alien and, above all, contemptuous view they took of our hominiform appearance, our anthropoid conformation, our condition as foetuses dropped prematurely into the deserts of the world, and thereafter crying out unceasingly with the same howl of anguish that announced our arrival on earth.

The discoveries of Freud and the Freudians would, without question, have fascinated the Gnostics, for all their cosmology and their anthropology bears the scars of this cosmic traumatism caused by man's *premature* appearance on earth. The error of the angels, the recklessness and clumsiness of those who sought to reproduce a model of the luminous archetype that sprang from the intellect of the true God, resulted in a veritable abortion being practised upon matter that was still virgin and in a state of pure gestation. For what they created was not a man but a shapeless worm, a foetus still unfit for life, and one cannot help wondering why the true God

34

decided to keep it alive. Beneath the complexity, the tortuousness of the Gnostic myths lies hidden this obvious truth: we are all premature births.

I believe that the whole of the Gnostics' ulterior attitude to man, society, the human race, and the mechanism of the cosmos, is founded on this primary vision (one could even say this imago) of the origin of man, forever scarred by his inherent immaturity. We are chrysalids snatched prematurely from our protective cocoons. Besides, the very term Gnosticism—*gnosis*—is very close, in Greek, to *genesis*, which means birth and origin. Gnosticism is, in essence, a genesis, it *restores to man his true birth, and overcomes his genetic and mental immaturity.*

To the history of man's creation, as summarized above, we must add another version, derived from the Valentinians, a sect who carried on the teachings of the Gnostic Valentinus in Egypt. It shows how profoundly Gnostic myths—in spite of widely differing variants—are haunted by this first moment.

The cosmology of the Valentinians reiterates the systems already described, but it adds several revealing details. At the summit, or, if you prefer, at the intelligible centre of the universe, is the good God, the stranger God. Below, descending in tiers down to our own terrestial world, are thirty circles, each guarded by an Aeon. All this, according to Valentinus, constitutes the Pleroma, that is to say, the world of Plenitude, the reservoir of Essences. The Aeon of the thirtieth circle was called Sophia ('Wisdom'). Now one day Sophia desired to contemplate the splendour of the Pleroma. It was an ill-fated wish. As soon as she crossed the last circle, light dazzled her, she was seized with vertigo and fell down to our world.

This myth is not entirely of Gnostic origin. In the legend of Semele, the Greeks had already expressed the feeling that man is neither ready nor able to bear the blinding vision of plenitude. Semele, mistress of Zeus, who visits her incognito at night, begs him one day to reveal himself, to appear to her in all his glory. Zeus warns her but Semele will not be put off; the unhappy woman wants to see the 'real' visage of her lover at all costs. Finally Zeus manifests himself in the light of his divine radiance and Semele, struck by lightning, falls to the earth. As she is pregnant, Zeus opens her belly, takes out the foetus and inserts it in his thigh, where he incubates it until the full term. Thus is born Dionysus, offspring of the Lightning and of a female who was too inquisitive.

As in the case of Semele, Sophia's brief intrusion into the splendours of the Pleroma was not without sequel: she was made pregnant by the Plenitude, the Numinous, and gave birth to a creature. I say creature, for this being, born of a glimpse of a forbidden world, had all the characteristics of an inhuman monster—so inhuman, indeed, that its own mother dared not even look at it or touch it.

It was from this monster that man was born, after certain modifications, corrections, additions, and retouchings had been carried out with the help of the Aeons of the Pleroma. In short, here too— and in a neater and more poignant version than in the other myths —the Gnostics have described the horrific origin of the first man. Happily, something of that brief contemplation of the glory on high, which set his birth in motion, survives within him as a reflection of the Invisible, described in a Gnostic text as 'something like a colour, a touch of light,' which deposited an emulsion of divine light on the dark background of our psyche.

These fascinating and nightmarish myths tend, therefore, to explain both our arrival in the world and the nature of our limitations and imperfections. One would not exist without the other, for it is precisely because of this premature or parthenogenetic birth, this unnatural conception, that we are cursed with a heavy, opaque body and a slumbering psyche, but also blessed with a spark of the divine light. And the consequences of this duality, of this refinement carried out at the last moment on a living abortion of matter, are visible in the body itself. Everything in man predestines him to be an obstacle to the expansion of light; a prison in which the desires of the psyche beat helplessly against the limitations of the being; a tomb in which we daily celebrate our own funeral rites. It is not only these forms, these anatomical structures, these organs of sense—ears, eyes, and taste buds that perceive only a fraction of the sound waves, the light rays, and the savours of the cosmos— it is not only our skeletal, nervous, and circulatory systems that condition us unjustly (because they limit our perceptive field), but our whole physiology, the very exercise of the vital organic and psychic functions which clouds and obscures our lives.

By way of example, let us again take nutrition, the first of the constraints imposed on man. We know that it extends the field of death *ad infinitum.* If man were not obliged to nourish himself by slaughtering other species; if, like the plants, he could sustain life by purely chemical exchanges with his environment, by an uninterrupted cycle of absorptions and restitutions, by metamorphoses instead of destruction and devouring—who knows whether the entire history of the human race might not have been altered? Wars, for example, would become pointless, or at the most very secondary. No Gnostic seems to have had this idea (which appears absurd on the surface), or, at any rate, none expressed it clearly, but I am sure that it is a logical expression of their line of questioning. The order of evil, which is the inherent order of this world, affirms itself through the constant necessity of destroying and devouring, a necessity so widespread, so planetary, that it places war and nutrition on an identical plane. Seen in this perspective, wars are nothing but an inescapable means by which communities feed themselves and survive.

Nutrition has another natural consequence: defecation, the logical conclusion of corporeal corruption. Defecation is a natural evil of the heavy, dense body, the plainest symbol of our wallowing in primordial slime. This, then, is the origin of the curious—but perfectly logical—notion that the bodies of those who attain a higher state of consciousness, which may be interpreted as a lightening of their matter, must be liberated from such scandalous servitude. The Gnostic Valentinus affirms quite naturally, therefore, that Jesus 'ate and drank but did not defecate. Such was the strength of his continence that foods did not become corrupt in him, for in him there was no corruption.'

And so, our organic portrait is simple: this talking foetus, this rectified worm that is man, cannot survive without destroying the life around him (like a worm gnawing the rotten wood of old beams) and expelling through his anus the corrupted products of this corrupting massacre. He absorbs filth through one end and rejects it in a still more corrupt state through the other.

What means exist, then, for breaking this lumbriciform cycle,

for wrenching oneself free of the mentality of a qualified amphib-
ian and shattering the vile mirror that eternally throws back our
own reflection and hides from us the true splendours of the hyper-
world? It is possible to reject the beguiling trickery of the world by
abstaining from procreation, and the majority of Gnostics did this,
refusing to insert the absurd parenthesis of life between prenatal
nothingness and death. It is more difficult to abstain from feeding
oneself. All ascetic disciplines, no matter how austere, involve a
minimum of nourishment. The greatest saints defecated, just like
everyone else. One might, therefore, think of a simpler and more
radical solution: suicide. But this solution is the absolute antithesis
of the Gnostic attitude. Not one of them, at any time, preached
suicide. The aim of the Gnostic is not the conjugate extinction of
life and of consciousness, but the mastering of the one and the
other, the attainment of a hyper-life and a hyper-consciousness.
For within man himself there exists a proof that all is not lost, and
that he possesses, within his very body, evidence of his partially
divine origin. Just as the constellations, those glittering perforations in the cosmic tissue, prove the existence of another world, so,
similarly, there exists in the tissue of our cells a perforation through
which we can see the spark of life shining. And this perforation is
the pupil of the eye.

The eye. Like the mouth, the anus and the navel, those three
bodily apertures that make man the site of exchanges between the
external world and the internal world of his body—being foci of
absorption, rejection, and genesis—the eye is also an aperture. But
it is the only one in the entire body whose exchanges with the
external world escape corruption, as well as the law of entropy. It
is the only one which lives on light while the rest of the body is
sustained entirely by filth.

Let us examine the eye. It is round, globular; it resembles the
universe as described by the Gnostics. Within this orb are set three
successive circles, the eyeball (in its strict sense), the iris, and the
pupil. The exterior circle is that of the white, where the small
arteries and veins ramify like filamentous nebulae. The intermediary circle is the iris, speckled with contorted pigments which
show configurations, blots, and patterns. Finally, there is the
central circle of the pupil, the abyss of shadows wherein one may

glimpse the depths of the soul and the reflection of that luminous emulsion which is the matrical trace of the divine light. Thus the eye very naturally reproduces the pattern of the universe: the sub-lunar circle of the pupil, the median circle of the galactic world, the exterior circle of the extra-galactic world. To look at the human eye is to grasp the pattern of the entire universe. To contemplate the eye, and lose oneself in this dark well, as if in the heart of the great ocean depths shot through with phosphorescent flashes, is to seize the ultimate nature of our existence in this world, the magical point at which man and god meet and are united.

Here again, I am doing no more than extrapolating the senti-ments, or rather the presentiments, of the Gnostics. For this medi-tation which led them alternately to study the heavenly bodies and sound the mystery of the eye, this question addressed to the stars in the skies and the stars in men's eyes, gave them an inkling of the fundamental unity between the human finitude and the divine infinitude. Both one and the other are made of the same matter and contain the same spark. Therein—and *only* therein—lies the way, the sign, the message which allows man to entertain a hope of liberation. And so this investigation, begun in the nocturnal immensities of the infinite hyper-world, naturally conducts us back to the infinite smallness of the human eyeball, to man himself, com-pound of light and darkness, mud and flame, a microcosm torn between conflicting entities, a net which has retained, in the form of a spark, the fragile souvenir of his abortive birth.

History, Men, Sects

I lived in this world of darkness for myriads
of years and no one ever knew that I was
there.

GNOSTIC HYMN

For me, it is perpetual pain and shadow and
the dark night of the soul, and I have no
voice to cry out with.

ANTONIN ARTAUD
Fragments d'un Journal d'Enfer

V

THE HIGHROADS OF SAMARIA

Thou and I are but one.

SIMON MAGUS

No sooner was Gnostic thought born than it began to be disseminated along the great routes of the Orient, and, during the first two centuries of our era, its message was expressed by a multitude of sects, communities and thinkers. Geographically speaking, primitive Gnosticism developed in the same places as dawning Christianity and the Judaic religions: Palestine, Syria, Samaria and Anatolia. It was here, in these lands of apocalypse and revelation, in this crucible of all the Messianisms, in this cradle of arcane and mystical communities like the Essenes, that the first Gnostic thinkers appeared. If today we find it difficult to visualize them clearly, for want of a name, it is because their history is clouded with the very opacity and injustice they themselves denounced as inherent flaws in earthly matter. We know the Gnostics and their teachings mainly through the Fathers of the Church, whose only concern was to cover them with ridicule and condemn them as heretics.

Of Gnostic thought or thoughts, of the prodigious systems constructed by various dedicated and truth-seeking men, nothing remains, therefore, but fragments.* How much authentic and objective knowledge of the political theories of Trotsky, of Makhno or Rosa Luxemburg would we possess today if the only surviving records were a few more or less complete quotations from the official history of the Soviet Communist Party, under a chapter heading: 'On renegades and deviationist traitors'? That is virtually the position we are in with the Gnostics, but for some very rare

---

* See the Bibliographical Notes at the end of this book for the textual sources of Gnosticism.

texts discovered in the last century and a more recent collection
which came to light in the caves of Upper Egypt after the last war.
Even if the extracts quoted by certain Church Fathers seem fair,
and reveal a sincere desire to understand Gnosticism, the fact
remains that these quotations have been chosen with the specific
aim of denouncing the whole teaching, and so cannot be other than
partial and partisan.

Admittedly, all's fair in war, but one must add an equally important fact: the incompatability—the abyss, even—which separates Gnostic thought and sensibility from those of Christianity. In
spite of the borrowings from the Gospels which some Gnostics
indulged in, and various 'stale whiffs' of Christianity discernible
in others, they took their authority from a fundamentally different
teaching and culture. Here, it is no longer a problem of orthodoxy,
or of deviation from dogma, but a simple problem of comprehension or incomprehension. All the Christian writers feel—and
with justice—that the Gnostics are not their 'brothers,' that they
are adepts of a different religion, and this feeling only grows
stronger with the passage of the centuries. If the philosophy of a
Basilides or a Valentinus could pass, at a pinch, as being fairly close
to that of Christianity, the beliefs which their latter-day descendants, the Cathars, introduced into Southern France ten centuries
later, no longer had anything in common with Catholic orthodoxy.

However, in its beginnings, in these first centuries when Christianity itself was fighting for its survival and seeking its own path,
Gnosticism could still create the illusion that it was a Christian
doctrine. It could do so on two essential counts: first, because of its
content, since it borrowed a number of elements from the teaching
of the Apostles and the texts of the Gospels; second, in its form, for
in the early days it was preached by men who, like the Apostles,
travelled the highroads of Samaria, Palestine, Syria and Anatolia,
and, in many places, came into direct confrontation with the
disciples of Jesus.

The most ancient of these wandering Gnostic prophets is known to
history as Simon Magus. Since my purpose here is not to indulge in
exegetical studies of the sources of Gnosticism, I will spare the

reader details of the documents used by historians to define, or dispute, the image of this remarkable personage. Besides, for some of these historians it is debatable whether Simon Magus should be included amongst Gnostic preachers: for them, he was not a Gnostic at all.

[As I write, or rather reproduce, this sentence, I am compelled to ask myself what it really means. Gnosticism can be defined in a dozen different ways, so for the sentence to have meaning, one would have to adhere to a single definition and exclude all those whose teaching deviates from it. An absurd method which might, perhaps, suit the traditional religions based on a clearly established dogma, on canonical texts, and orthodox interpretations, but which, specifically, cannot be applied to Gnosticism, whose most incontestable aim is to break down the arbitrary frontiers established by dogma, and to call upon the most diverse sources and teachings (Manicheism, Judaism, Greek philosophy, Christianity, Hermetism) for its own basic concepts, and to promote an open synthesis, new channels of reflection, an original mode of thinking, in short, precisely to escape the constriction of dogmatic definitions.]

To come back to Simon Magus (who was a native of Gitta, a small town in Samaria), two features characterize his life and his teaching: he travels the roads in the company of a woman called Helen, a former prostitute whom he found in a brothel in Tyre, and he declares, by turns, that he is the Sun and Helen the Moon, that he is Zeus and she Athene, and that he is the Supreme Power and she is Ennoia (Sophia), Wisdom descended from the heavens, the Mother of the universe.

And so the Father and Mother of the universe tramp the roads, preach, convert and, as the Acts of the Apostles attest, amaze the crowds by the miracles and the prodigious feats they perform. This takes place exactly seventeen years after the death of Jesus. The new world, born on the eastern shores of the Roman Empire, is still in its infancy. Everything has been said but nothing has taken on concrete form. At the very most, there are several dozen men— former disciples of Jesus or new converts to what is still no more than a miniscule group amongst so many others—preaching a new faith, a new god, an austere and radical teaching on the roads of

Palestine, Samaria and Anatolia. It is the era of prophets, Messiahs, gods incarnate and celestial envoys. Never has God had so many Sons upon the planet as at this time. The pagan authors, in astonished and ironic tones, describe this multitude of envoys suddenly descended upon earth, all of whom preach along the highways in identical terms: 'I am God, or I am the Son of God, or I am the Power of the Father or the Son. The end of Time is at hand. I have come to save you. Those who listen to me and follow me will gain eternal life. The rest will perish or burn in the fires of hell.'

Simon Magus is only one prophet among many, but he draws the crowds, they listen to him, follow him. The Apostles, who preach in the same squares, in the same villages, also have their listeners and their followers. But what Simon has to say is radically different from the Apostolic teaching. He brings with him a re-markable message, but—not having lived in that epoch—I cannot say whether he himself conceived it, taking his inspiration solely from previous teachings, or whether he had it intact from some unknown and now forgotten predecessor. And this message can be distinguished from all the others, for it is coherent, rational, and subversive as well—the Gnostic message *par excellence*. Here, then, is what Simon Magus taught:

On reading the Bible, and especially Genesis, one learns that Yahweh, Jehovah, or Elohim, in short the God of the Jews, is the author of this world. Now how does this God spend his time? Per-secuting man and the human race. He creates Adam, then Eve, sets them down in Paradise, but immediately forbids them the one essential: knowledge of Good and Evil. After this, and having chased the first human couple out of Paradise, he hounds their descendants unremittingly, multiplying the laws of prohibition, threatening the human species with the lightning of his wrath until the day when, with the Flood, he will wipe them out. But still it is not enough, and once again he showers the second humanity, the children of Noah, with fire, blood and calamity. He is a God of justice, a cosmic Policeman whose intransigent authoritarianism antagonizes even the angels, and who never intervenes in earthly matters except to thwart human evolution.

In arguing thus, Simon does not question or doubt the reasons for this aggressive behaviour. He does not deny man's errors or his crimes, but declares simply that this image of an avenging God, ruthlessly hammering mankind, is incompatible with the idea of a good God, the friend of man and creator of life. From this he concludes that since this world and its humanity, inaugurated in blood and crime, are patently the work of Jehovah, the latter cannot be the true God, but is a false god or simply a demiurge, that sadistic and perverse demiurge depicted in the Bible as a touchy, vindictive, choleric, jealous and evil being.

It goes without saying that such teaching flew in the face of the whole Apostolic doctrine and the teaching of Jesus. This outright rejection of the Revelation must have appeared, in its time, not only revolutionary but scandalous, impious, and inadmissible. Nevertheless, Simon continued to preach and seek in the Biblical texts themselves clear proofs of the subversion of the world by the God of Genesis. His cosmology, in so far as it can be gathered from the extracts quoted by the Fathers of the Church, reveals a scrupulously rational thinker, equally scrupulous in seeking a liberating path for mankind. For it seems to him impossible, too unjust, intolerable, that man should have to pay the price of Jehovah's ambition. There must be something within him that enables him to conceive of, and to rediscover, the true God, the God who is a stranger to this world. Thus Simon builds up a seductive doctrine, a framework in which to review the possible nature and destiny of man.

Man, in his eyes, is flawed only in his functioning. His hominid forms, his mental and organic structures, even his essential being, are not inherently evil, for in spite of Jehovah's tampering, man is still a miniature projection of the universe created in thought by the true God, and carries within himself the imprint of the real world. Simon sees a proof of this in the story of man's creation in Eden, as related in Genesis. Paradise, the Garden of Eden, is the matrix from which man is born, the umbilicus of life from which the human species springs. This term 'umbilicus' must be taken here in its proper sense. For if man is the universe on a reduced scale, it follows that the universe is a man on an aggrandized scale, a giant Anthropos. Everything that is to be found in the sky has its double or its reflection in man or on the earth. Eden is the living matrix that nourishes our earth, and the River that irrigates it feeds the clay from which man was drawn; this River divides into four primordial streams which Simon recognizes as the four arteries—two of air and two of blood—which irrigate and feed man's circulatory and respiratory systems. Man carries the rivers of Eden in his body as he carries the truly divine spark in his psyche. He contains, in a reduced and potential form, the living forces, the creative seeds which are also those of the universe, and whose first, unifying force is fire.

Simon thought a great deal about fire and its multiple forms—igneous, incandescent, tepid, cooled (he was the first to dream of cold fire, an idea which so many alchemists came back to later)—and its presence at the heart of the human body. Two forms of divine fire exist in man: a psychic form which is desire—notably the desire to beget—and a physical form which is blood. Blood, like fire, is red and warm, it is a fire which circulates through the body of man, diminished, to be sure, but lukewarm and stable (an organicist conception of the Simonian universe would give a very sound explanation of the temperature and homothermy of mammals); it subdivides into two complementary fires: semen in the male and milk in the female. If man possesses the power to beget, it is because he carries within him the psychic fire of desire and the physical fire of blood and semen.

For Simon, this image of man as a brazier in which the divine fire circulates in a cooled and diminished state implies a number of consequences, one of which seems to me worth noting, for at the time it opened up a totally different way from that preached in the Gospels. Man is endowed with a fragment of divine fire. Good. It is this which gives him a special status among all living beings, and confers on him the privileges of reason, language, and an upright posture. But these privileges, although innate, are not eternal. They are more in the nature of possibilities, or aptitudes, dependant on the individual, and the conditions in which he lives, for their development or disappearance.

To make this idea comprehensible, Simon offers us a telling example. Our psyche, he says, is potentially capable of conceiving and practising speech, grammar, and geometry. But if these human aptitudes are not developed—and today we would add *developed soon enough*—they will be lost forever and no one will even know that man possesses them. It is immediately clear that this idea of a certain 'terrain' necessary to the development of aptitudes has implications which go well beyond the strictly religious and theological domain. Out of all Simon's listeners who possessed a congenital aptitude for grammar and geometry, how many effectively realized them in the course of their lives? And surely the drama becomes still more crucial when this handicap is also applied to man's chances of immortality—particularly for the people of that era, who believed the end of the world to be imminent. For the psyche possesses a specific aptitude for immortality, just as it does for speech, grammar, and geometry. And, like the other aptitudes, its fate is bound up with the attitude the individual adopts towards it. In other words, *the soul is not immortal by nature, it can only become so* if man feeds and sustains this privileged fire which he carries within him. Otherwise, ineluctably, he will return to nothingness.

One need hardly underline the extent to which this doctrine contradicted the preaching of the Apostles. For them, man's soul is immortal, no matter what he may do, and his fate condemns him to burnish it or tarnish it, to know the delights of paradise or the torments of hell, throughout eternity. For the Gnostic, the die is cast *here, before death.* Which is why he feels this sense of anguish in the face of time and the brevity of the human span, a feeling that is so characteristic of the Gnostic sensibility, and one which is only remotely related to the melancholy Jeremiads of the poets who lament the passing of the days: every moment of our lives is counted, for each is a door opening on to immortality or the void.

Here then, in the very first years of our era, the fundamental certitudes which will unceasingly sustain Gnostic contemplation are set out: the world we live in was not created by the true God, it is the work of an impostor, and man's task will consist in rejecting the swindle of this world, together with the Biblical and Christian teaching which claims to uphold it and all the institutions through which it is perpetuated. Thus, from the start, the Gnostic identi-. fies himself as a marginal creature, forced (by the historical evolution of society as well as by his own inclinations) to form alternative and secret communities which will transmit the Teaching.

And as the second aspect of this Teaching, consequent upon the first principle: man is called upon, in this struggle against the generalized oppressiveness of the real, *to create a soul for himself,* or if you prefer, to nourish, fortify, and enrich the luminous spark he carries in his innermost being. It remains for us to discover how Simon translated these aspirations into concrete terms, and here again we shall find a typically Gnostic attitude applied to the options of daily life.

Simon lived with Helen, a woman described by some Christian authors as a former prostitute. According to Simon (and no doubt to herself, too), this Helen was the divine Wisdom come down to earth. The Christian writers, of course, sneer at this claim. To pose as the Father and Mother of the universe, to pass themselves off as Zeus and Athene, or the Sun and the Moon, could only be a joke, or a deliberate provocation. But in fact, it is known that such claims were common at the time, and Simon by no means had the monopoly. Therefore, what seems more significant is that he appears to be the only one of all the 'Gods' or 'Envoys' of his epoch to live openly with a concubine and form a couple. And it is precisely through this couple, and in this couple, that his teaching is embodied.

In Simon's view, semen, which issues from the divine fire in man, and desire, the psychic fire which causes it to be emitted from his body, are the chosen means of man's liberation. In opposition to the Bible's truncated image of the couple, where the woman is made out of the man and not coexistent with him, Simon offers us the image of a primordial couple with the woman *existing at the same time* as the man whose destiny Jehovah foiled and who therefore could not come into being. It is he, Simon, and she, Helen, who through a mutual desire for the fusion of their bodies and their souls will re-establish the primary order of the world, who will fulfil the message of desire 'intercepted' by Jehovah. Make love, says Simon, as a way of combatting the world's confusion, of restoring desire to its rightful and essential place, and of fuelling the generative fire which is also blood, milk, and semen.

Here again, one can imagine how this teaching—anodyne to

pagans, no doubt—must have outraged ears already tuned to
Christianity. For it seems that some thirty or so disciples were
gathered around Simon and Helen, all living in freely united
couples, and it is even more than probable that these couples
practised free love among themselves, as other Gnostic sects were to
do later on. What the Christian authors in every case quite erron-
eously call the 'Simonian mysteries,' boil down, then, to the
practice of free love with no attempt to prevent the begetting of
children. Later Gnostics were to adopt the totally opposite path
of ascetism, or a refusal to procreate. But here we see one of the
features of Gnosticsm that singled it out from the very beginning:
the ambivalence of all behaviour. The radical attitude adopted
towards the flesh permits, *without prejudice or preference,* the
exercise of a rigorous asceticism or an equally rigorous 'debauchery,' for both are roads leading to liberation.

For Simon, at any rate, the fecundation of women is no hind-
rance to the salvation of the world, provided that it takes place outside the framework of the institutions which since time immemorial
have aimed at controlling, regimenting and perverting its true
meaning. This practice of free love must be the means of burst-
ing out of the social straitjacket specifically invented to stifle its
liberating spontaneity. The Christian author Hippolytus of Rome
reports—and was no doubt scandalized by—this relevant saying
of Simon and his disciples: 'All soil is but soil, and what matters it
where one sows? In the promiscuity of men and women lies the
true communion.'

It would be wrong to read into this phrase what we call today 'an
incitement to debauchery' or a 'perversion of adults.' For this communion, which intermingles seeds, desires, and living beings, while
breaking all ties of an institutional and probably also of a sentimental nature, aims at a sort of fusion, a first victory over this world
whose deepest nature is one of separation, division, dispersal
through the weight of matter. To struggle against all that divides
and erodes, to reassemble the scattered sparks in each one of us, to
close up the gulf that separates human beings from one another as
surely as it separates humanity as a whole from the heavens—in
short, to dismantle the circles set up by the demiurge to keep each
of us in helpless solitude—this undoubtedly is what Simon's phrase

meant in the eyes of the initiated. At this stage, in fact, individual-ities disappear along with the first of all prisons, that of the I. To break down the I, to melt into the Thou, into the He (and here, one again discovers the particular importance Simon gave to grammar, whose rigid categories were among thousands of revealing examples of the alienating splitting-up of the elements that make up the world), to remove the very categories of I, Thou, He, *and to become We,* such must be the meaning of the so-called 'mysteries of the Simonians.' 'Thou and I are but one,' said Simon in a lost work entitled *The Great Relevation of a Voice and a Name.*

For the rest, we are left with nothing but legends, the anecdotes reported by the Christian Fathers regarding the life and death of Simon Magus. They are legends nevertheless worth telling for they reveal the concern already felt by Christians, and their efforts to discredit the Gnostics under the guise of authenticity. Many miracles and prodigies were attributed to Simon Magus. The Acts of the Apostles, the most ancient Christian text in which he is men-tioned, already reports: 'But there was a certain man, called Simon, which beforetime in the same city used sorcery and be-witched the people of Samaria, giving out that himself was some great one: To whom they all gave heed, from the least to the great-est, saying, This man is the great power of God. And to him they had regard, because that of long time he had bewitched them with sorceries.'

This following of Simon's among the population of Samaria— and of Rome, later on, when he repaired to that city—consider-ably hampered the preaching of the Apostles. For Simon competed with them on their own ground, and Peter himself, according to the apologist Justin, was several times compelled to follow in his foot-steps, to preach against him and disabuse prospective Christians. This is no doubt the source of the anecdote in the Acts which relates how Simon, on seeing the Apostles Peter and John bring down the Holy Spirit upon the faithful by a simple laying-on of hands, offered them money to purchase the same power. Hence the term *Simony,* which has become common usage since then, and which is defined in the *Dictionnaire de Droit Canonique* as: 'The premeditated attempt to buy or sell for a worldly price that which is intrinsically spiritual.' The anecdote could be true. But what it implies—and this is why it originated—is that Simon had only false powers, he was nothing but a common charlatan. It is this image which the subsequent legends are at pains to foster, notably on the subject of his death.

At the time, two different versions of his death were in circulation. In one, Simon, during the course of his sojourn in Rome, was arguing with the Apostle Peter who denied that he had any real power. Simon declared that he could fly up to the sky. Peter challenged him; Simon immediately took flight. But Peter uttered a prayer which caused him to fall to the ground, where he broke into four pieces and died. Let us record, in passing, that the Christian writers who reported this tale (in which they firmly believed), do not appear at any moment to have reproached Peter for using prayer as a means to commit pure and simple murder. But we will let that pass. In the other version, Simon's death occurred thus: he was sitting under a plane-tree arguing with the Apostles and, here again, boasting of his powers. 'I can rise from the dead like Jesus Christ,' he declared, 'bury me and I will rise again in three days.' The Apostles accepted the challenge, shut Simon up in a coffin and buried him at the foot of the tree. They waited three days: Simon did not rise again.

So ended—in the air or under the earth—the life of one who had violently opposed the apostolic teaching and sewn confusion along the highroads of Samaria. His teaching did not disappear with him. One can only infer that his contemporaries were not at all convinced by these tales of a Gnostic Icarus, or a false Christ buried alive, for a certain number continued to follow his message. The essential point about everything concerning Simon Magus is that, with him, Gnosticism declares its originality, its power to fascinate, from its position on the fringes of traditional teaching and preaching, and that it presents a face that will remain uniquely its own during the following centuries. This face is that of the primordial Couple, it is the face of Desire—Desire aflame, Desire run wild—exalted as the primary fire of the world and the source of liberation, and it is the face of Wisdom, incarnate in the body of Helen, who has fallen from the heights of heaven into the depths of history to teach men that the way to salvation is through fecundating that reflection of the divine splendour—the body of a woman.

VI

THE MASTERS OF GNOSIS

The perpetration of any voluptuous act whatever is a matter of indifference.

BASILIDES

Make death die.

VALENTINUS

How does an idea make its 'way,' as it is called? By what meandering channels, what individual tributaries (which do not always return to the mainstream, although they are fed by it), does it manage to insinuate itself here and there, disappearing suddenly to spring up again, equally suddenly, somewhere else? This question may appear trivial or merely academic, and yet I maintain that as far as Gnosticism is concerned no historian has given us a serious answer. It is curious to note that, when it comes to causality, even competent and thoughtful men will sometimes lull themselves into complacency with superficial and misleading explanations. For example, Robert Grant, a recent historian of Gnosticism and author of a remarkable work entitled *Gnosticism and Early Christianity,* explains certain analogies between Buddhist philosophy and that of Basilides the Gnostic as follows: 'It is certainly possible that at Alexandria Basilides could have acquired some knowledge of Buddhism from Indian merchants and traders.' Without underestimating the philosophic knowledge of merchants — Indian or otherwise — I do not see how a man like Basilides, whose writings reveal a profound knowledge of the various religions of his time, could have owed his subsequent borrowings from Buddhism to such men. It is rather as if, some centuries from now, a historian (if they still exist) were to explain

54

Teilhard de Chardin's knowledge of Peking Man (Sinanthropus) in these words: 'He would have been able to acquire this information from the members of some Chinese trade delegation visiting Europe at the time when he was writing *Le Phénomène Humain.*' One must realize that the majority of historical works, including those of the highest repute, are full of statements of this kind.

The reason I have asked myself this question is because it seems clear, on one hand, that Simon Magus's teaching did not die with him (it was carried on in Samaria, Syria and possibly Egypt), and on the other, that it was transmitted in a clandestine and underground fashion, which makes it difficult to trace by irrefutable documentation. We shall find the same thing when we come to the other leading figures of Gnosticism, whose works—lost to us today —were secret even during their own lifetimes, because of their content (which was reserved for certain initiates) and also because of the need to elude prosecution and the harassment of the Christians. This is why we are relatively ignorant about the Gnostics except for the period in which they found themselves, along with the Christians, in the position of outlaws or rebels against the Roman authority, that is to say, throughout the second century. The internal dissensions between true and false Christians could not at that time lead to the outright extermination or excommunication of one sect by the other. The presence and the power of the common enemy forced them to postpone this 'settling' of differences till a later date. It is true that the history of the Russian revolution and, still more, the recent history of revolutionary parties in Europe, has taught us that even when faced by a common and powerful enemy — Tsarism or Capitalism — revolutionary groups or splinter-groups will not give up their internal quarrels. But this is for a very simple reason: the liberalism of Western societies tolerates these divisions and, indeed, makes use of them. If a successful revolution were to take place tomorrow and one of these groups seized power, we know quite well that such tolerance would no longer be the order of the day; the only recourse for the ousted party would be exile or a clandestine existence. And just as it is impossible to imagine Trotskyite or Maoist groups being officially recognized in a People's Democracy, so the Christian accession to power rendered the survival of the Gnostics extremely precarious. In fact, it is precisely at this period, during the fourth century, that they vanish from the pages of history—which does not mean they ceased to exist—and the teachings and writings of the Gnostic masters become wholly illicit. And so we see superimposed on the tragedy of human fate, another which nourishes and confirms it: the tragedy of history itself, that terrestrial measure of cosmic time —time, which, for the Gnostics, was always the most significant sign of our alienation.

This is why a history of the Gnostic movement cannot possibly be written like a traditional history. It is in a sense a shadow-history, a counter-history whose successive pages make a desperate attempt to deny history itself, to rescue man from the treadmill of time's passing. From the earliest decades of our era, the most farsighted, or the most convinced Christians had the feeling that they were founding a new era—albeit one that would be constantly threatened by the end of time — overthrowing the old ways of the world and constructing a new man, whereas the Gnostics never at any time, either in their writings or in their silences, showed the least concern to leave lasting traces on this earth. We can see that this is obvious, a logical consequence of their entire outlook. They laugh at posterity, perenniality, the future, and all those snares and pitfalls of time in which man allows himself to be caught. What the Gnostics preach is immediate flight, a desertion of the world and the demarcations of time. How then can one write the history of those who specifically rejected it, how can one capture the likeness of constantly fleeing shadows? One can pursue the Gnostics, but one cannot seize hold of them. And, in any case, the very act of seizing them would be a violation. What would a Basilides, a Valentinus, or a Carpocrates say if he were to look down from the lofty heights of the hyper-world (where no doubt he now resides) and read this book today? That I myself have fallen into the trap of time, I am caught in the talons of history, and that — no matter how laudable my intentions or sympathetic my attitude—I am but adding a useless and deceptive book to the density of time. I could offer only one hypothesis which might, at a pinch, mitigate their verdict: that I am a Gnostic, reincarnated after two thousand years. But even this hypothesis does not entirely absolve me from blame, for if I am living on this earth in the 1970s, it means that I am still subject to the cycle of reincarnation—in which many of them believed—and have not purged myself of material servitude nor liberated the spark of life from its bodily prison. In short, I have not totally received gnosis. If I had, I would be in the splendour of the Pleroma, freed from matter, speech, mental and psychic categories, from history, time and, above all, from the trouble of thinking anything at all about them. From the pure and austere Gnostic viewpoint, then, this book is absurd. For it claims to intervene in a world of non-intervention. It violates non-violence. It operates like those crude means of observation employed by physicists to study the structures of the atom and which, since they are inevitably made of natural matter themselves (light, rays, bundles of particles), disturb and even destroy the object they are seeking to observe. Studying Gnosticism with the mental means at our disposal involves, to some extent, disturbing and destroying it.

Logic demands, therefore, that I stop here and now. But, apart from my contractual obligations to my publisher, something deeper urges me to continue. The fact is, I feel a love for these men and for the silence they longed to melt into; moreover, I delight in the knowledge that today there is a sensibility, an attitude, an underground current characteristic of our time that seeks them out again and perpetuates them. The paradox of fate wills that non-history always follows history, that anti-societies presuppose societies. We are still haunted by the question: why, century after century, have men gathered together to say NO to something? This something has taken on ever-changing forms—predominantly political in the last fifty years—but, by the same token, even our awareness, and our protest, are fragmented. This is the first unwritten law of alienation, and we need to be conscious of it: the something we say NO to is never the real enemy, but only the shadow it casts over us and within us.

After the death of Simon Magus, a certain number of disciples carried on his teaching. The names of two of these are known to us: Menander and Saturninus. Disciples, however, is too strong a term. Each in fact followed his own way, taking inspiration from the guide-lines laid down by Simon but pushing them further towards completion or even deviating from them. For Gnosticism itself teaches us not to hold on to those false criteria by which the history of ideas is ultimately written. Having possessed neither churches nor dogma nor ecclesiastical councils, Gnosticism was able to develop along multiple paths, all of which form part of the whole. Unlike the history of Christianity, which is always the story of dogma triumphing over heresy, Gnostic history must take account of all the different currents and guard against favouring one to the detriment of others. There is no such thing as a heresy in Gnosticism, it is unthinkable for Gnosticism is essentially an embodying and not a dividing force.

And so Menander and Saturninus continued Simon's work but added their own meditations to it. Saturninus, who taught at Antioch nearly a century after the death of the master, seems to have gained a considerable following. It is to him that we owe among other things the detailed description of the creation of man given above, and it was he who applied the name of 'unknown Father' to the true God, stranger to this world. It seems that we also owe him the idea that the evil demiurges, the ignoble Aeons responsible for the world — and he named them the Archons — are none other than the seven planets.

Hebraic cosmology had already described the planets not as dead stars but as living beings, as archangels whose brilliance was supposedly a celebration of the glory of the All-Powerful. Gnosticism retains this vision but reverses its meaning: these living planets, these blazing archangels shine forth above us in celebration of their own glory. It is as usurpers that they occupy their domain of the lower heavens and rule over their damned creation. There is not a glimmer of admiration, of beatitude, in his eye as Saturninus turns his gaze upon the perversity of this absurdly starspangled heaven, habitat of those nocturnal malefactors and thieves of the soul which are the heavenly bodies. In the teeming multiplicity of the stars he saw the flaming grid that bars our terrestrial prison, and in the oppressive orbs of the planets the gaolers of our planetary detention.

But it is in Egypt, rather than in Syria, Palestine or Samaria, that Gnosticism comes to its fullest flowering. There we see it developing with prodigious speed from the beginning of the second century, that strange, confused century in which the great pulsations of history seem to throb like muffled drums, spawning gods, cults, conversions and recantations, especially in that city which was the geographical centre of all the confusion, but also the great wellspring of ideas: Alexandria.

Crucible, burning-glass, mortar and blast-furnace; the still wherein all heavens, all gods, all visions are mixed, distilled, infused and transfused: such was Alexandria in the second century. Look wherever you will, interrogate history from any standpoint or level whatever, and you will find all races represented there (except the Chinese, who have not yet arrived), all continents (Africa, Asia, Europe) and all ages (Ancient Egypt, whose sanctuaries are preserved there, the ages of Athens and Rome, of Judea, Palestine, and Babylon); all these elements are gathered together in this knot of the Delta, this city which is to the river what lungs are to men and branches to a tree: the place through which they breathe and the source of their inspiration.

Admittedly, this image only takes shape with hindsight. Strangers who journeyed to Alexandria at that time saw nothing at first but confusion, an indescribable mixture of beliefs and religious rites, anarchy, and the dissolution of all certainties. They felt that they were lost in some wasteland of history, entangled in the web of all these contradictions, engulfed by the whirlpool of these incompatible creeds. '. . . Here one can see Bishops, who claim to be Christians, paying homage to Serapis. There is not a single priest— Samaritan, Christian or Jew—who is not a mathematician, a haruspex or alypte. When the Patriarch himself comes to Egypt, he worships both Christ and Serapis to keep everybody happy . . . ,' writes the Emperor Hadrian to his friend, the Consul Servianus.

At just about the time of Hadrian's visit to the city—approximately 130 AD — we find several of the most renowned Gnostics teaching in Alexandria: Basilides, Carpocrates, Valentinus. Let us note one fact at the outset: although they travel from time to time, to Rome, Greece or Cyprus, they are no longer itinerant prophets. Henceforth, Gnosticism is established in the cities, above all in *the* City, Alexandria, where it finds a rich and fertile soil. For here all systems meet, rub shoulders or conflict with one another: Egyptian, Greek and Roman paganism, Coptic Christianity, Judaism, Neo-

Platonic philosophies, Hermetism, and still others, some of which mingle in ephemeral syncretisms, while others, notably the Christian sects, tend to split, break up, and separate. To the Gnostics, separation, division, and scattering are specifically terrestrial signs of alienation. Basilides, Carpocrates and Valentinus take whatever they find good from wherever they may find it. But it is not my intention here to look for the various sources and origins of Gnosticism. What matters in my eyes is not the source but the estuary, the outflow, the particular teaching of the great Gnostics. A doctrine like Gnosticism cannot be created, cannot be vivified simply by portioning out several ingredients borrowed from earlier systems, adding some excipient, mashing it up, and firing the whole mixture in the great kiln or crucible of Alexandria. All the research, all the books written on the question of the sources of Gnosticism have shed light on only one aspect of the problem: they have shown that Christianity, Judaism, Neo-Platonic philosophy, Stoicism, Epicureanism, Cynicism, and Hermetism have all served Gnosticism. But the point is: Gnosticism is *not* just a hastily put-together amalgam of systems. Once these first constituents are combined and fused together, Gnosticism itself is a new substance, a mutant thought, a creation which as soon as it is born outstrips and denies its origins. In fact, it does not hesitate to push its history to a logical conclusion and deny itself.

Thus Basilides, one of the first Alexandrian masters of Gnosticism, places Illusion at the origin and centre of the world, and at the heart of our own psyche, and proposes total Ignorance as a means of vanquishing it. We are dealing with a thought, a system, that goes so far in search of the No, the not, the non-being, the non-existent and the non-real that language itself is powerless to interpret it. For Basilides tells us 'there was a time when nothing was. When I say nothing, I do not mean that there *was* nothing, but simply, crudely, totally that nothingness itself did not exist.'

This dizzying nothingness—which one must nevertheless think of and write in order to say that nothing was, since by saying that I pose the existence of a something that was nothing—this dizzying nothingness of words in which thought immediately founders and sinks, waterlogged by these imperfect syllables, these omnipotent letters N-O-T-H-I-N-G, becomes still more bewildering when

Basilides sets out to analyse the negative implications of this nothing. 'Nothing, then, existed, neither matter nor substance nor beings without substance, nor simple beings nor compound beings, nor intelligible beings, nor sentient nor non-sentient beings, neither angel, nor man, nor god, nor absolutely any of the beings one can name or whom one perceives through the senses or through the intelligence.' To the point where God himself is called—curiously but with impeccable logic—He who is not.

But if God is He who is not and if nothing existed, how was the world made? Here again, one comes up against the prison-bars of words. 'He who is not,' Basilides goes on, 'wanted to make the world. I use the word "wanted" to make myself intelligible, but in fact there was no thought, no desire, no feeling. And the God who is not made the world of that which is not.'

At this stage, where thought struggles so incessantly against the treachery of language that a word is no sooner written than it is challenged and rejected, the world-process takes on unsuspected forms. How can one set oneself against that which is not? How can one live in the heart of a misunderstanding so total that everything which surrounds us is in reality non-real, a reflection, an illusion, a distorting mirror, a phantom? Here Basilides lifts the totality of the world to the level of a cosmic fantasy engendered by the planetary sleep of pseudo-living creatures. For only sleep can induce us to accept the dream for the reality. When Basilides says that the world is an illusion, he does not mean (I presume) that the world we live in does not exist—since it *is*—but that it exists in the form of an illusion. It is the mirage of another world as yet uncreated, unengendered, although it exists in a latent state in the non-brain of the non-God, and one asks oneself whether it is perhaps the appointed task of the Gnostics to bring it into being, to materialize this world by awakening the total consciousness of mankind, by fleeing from the mirage and stepping through the illusory looking-glass which is at once our earth and our sky.

Elsewhere, in a still more precise example, one can see how far Basilides' radicalism leads him. Certain ancient philosophers—Greeks and Christians—said that God is by nature ineffable. Not so, says Basilides, for to say that something is ineffable is to confer upon it an existence and a condition. 'There exist,' he explains, 'things which are not even ineffable and are therefore beyond any possible name.' And so, at the extreme limit of Basilides' thought, one quite naturally comes up against not the un-nameable but the impossibility of even envisaging it, in short, one encounters Silence.

Silence. Here we are at the very heart of Gnostic teaching. We know, through the testimony of Basilides' Christian adversaries, that he followed the example of Pythagoras by imposing a five-year silence on his disciples. Perhaps this silence was not limited to the disciples but included the master as well. Very little is known about Basilides and his school, and it is impossible to imagine exactly how he taught. But even if he was the only teacher to impose the ascetic discipline of silence, this fact is still revealing. Silence is one of the purest and most difficult ways of combatting the illusion of the world. For this silence is not merely the absence of sound, the cessation of words; it must be the means of awakening within the disciple—through the state of constant watchfulness that it implies —a heightened awareness, a firing-up of thought to strengthen the soul. Denial of speech leads to the triumph of hyper-consciousness. Abstention, like non-violence, becomes a weapon. One can already discern the practical paths Basilides' teaching is leading us to: since this world is made up of that which is not, we must fight against it by denying it, notably through silence. We will oppose the noises of this world, the ephemeral sound-waves of speech, the sonorous and falsely beguiling matter of the universe *by our silence, which then becomes a kind of anti-matter.*

And there is another weapon we shall use. The desire to know, to seek beyond the false and evanescent forms of the world and discover the true mechanisms which move them, is suspect. For surely knowledge itself, in a world of illusions, can only be illusory? The things we are enquiring into are mere reflections, day-dreams, wraiths. Logic itself becomes ineffectual, since it is the logic of vacuity. In most cases, it is nothing more than an idling motor, rotating pointlessly in that labyrinth of mirages which we call the human brain. It is only Ignorance, in conjunction with Silence, that can lead us down the royal road to liberation.

Admittedly, Basilides had to temper this total rejection of knowledge to some extent. Caught in the snare of these successive negations which reverberate within us, repeatedly echoing our doubts, he had to compromise. He is said to have written twenty-four books of commentaries on the Gospels, as well as some Odes, and to have initiated a mystical cult for his disciples—which obviously pre-supposes a knowledge of the mysteries. But he did not neglect what we may call 'practical advice.' It is not difficult to imagine the form this would have taken. Confronted with the deceptions of reality, the imposture of all Churches and institutions, the mummery of laws, creeds, and taboos, he proposes a very simple morality: non-morality. Thus, at the moment when the first persecutions are beginning against both Christians and Gnostics (the Romans seeing not the slightest difference between the two), Basilides declares that it is natural and necessary to abjure one's faith in order to escape them. In the same way, sexual desire should not be shackled by the conventions, which are aimed at channelling it into socially-acceptable patterns, but must be freely satisfied for its own sake, without sentimental or matrimonial attachments. Which does not mean that Basilides preached free sexual union as the sole remedy for man's sufferings. As far as he personally is concerned, he does not appear to have been a satyr intoxicated with women, those 'chosen vessels' as they are called in a Gnostic text. To the initiates, those who had undergone the ordeal of silence, he probably counselled asceticism. To others, ordinary disciples or simply listeners, he left the freedom to choose the path they judged best. Unlike almost all esoteric groups and mystical communities throughout the ages, the Gnostics did not, at first, lay down any ethical precepts or prohibitions. It seems that they aimed, rather, at leaving each man free to join the teaching while carrying on his own way of life, without being committed to either asceticism or non-asceticism. It is with Basilides, then, that we see the declaration of that lordly indifference to rules of conduct, that radical liberation from all institutionalized systems which so scandalized his contemporaries.

When one reads the Gnostic texts and their cosmologies peopled with Aeons, Archons, Gods who are not, the Unengendered, prim-ordial Couples, divisive circles, castrating planets, and ravaging fires, one comes across an apparent contradiction: on the one hand, these writings traverse familiar territory (that of mythology) and, like so many other texts, can always be reduced to a number of archetypes and all the psychoanalytical interpretations. But on the other hand, these fantastic systems, these organized hallucinations, these ingenious constructions which are often barely intelligible, have served as engine-bed and motivation for a coherent teaching and a remarkably homogenous morality — or non-morality, if you prefer. It is quite obvious that compared to Gnostic cogitations Genesis and the Gospels are dazzlingly clear and simple. What then is concealed behind this complexity, these perpetual subtleties which transform the history of the world into a chain of absurd tragedies, a series of obscure causes and effects, amid a vast array of Archons and Powers, Entities without number? Was it necessary to stage so many *coups de théâtre,* to indulge in so much weeping and gnashing of teeth, so many falls and so much repentance, such contrivance and perversity on the part of the Archons and the Aeons, in order to make this eminently simple statement: real life is elsewhere?

I admit I am uncertain how to answer this formidable question. However, I will make an attempt, for the sympathy and loyalty I owe to these men and their ideas spurs me on. I wish that my loyalty was total, or at least that it did not come to grief on those sibylline texts, which are often specious and always very tedious. But let us take a passage from Basilides' cosmology, quoted by Hippolytus of Rome and drawn from the essay on the creation of the world:

'Then did the Son of the great Archon illuminate the light of the Son of the Archon of the Hebdomad, as he himself had lit his own on high through contact with the Filiality; then was the Son of the Archon of the Hebdomad enlightened and straightway, at the first word, he was affrighted and confessed his fault.' What is immediately apparent in this passage (an extract, as I recall, from a much longer quotation), is the complexity, the rigmarole of sequences and successive causalities supposed to explain why and how a deviation, an error, slipped into the process of creation. The terms Basilides uses: Hebdomad (the totality of the seven lower circles), the Filiality (an emanation of the God who is not, consisting of three parts: one subtle, one dense, the third impure), are obscure nowadays but were relatively common in his day, and many thinkers, Gnostic or otherwise, used them at that time when speculating, for example, upon the human and divine nature of Christ. But here one is entitled to ask oneself whether this system — totally arbitrary as it may appear, or even the ravings of a delirious mind — is not, in fact, the reflection of those very mysteries, complex in themselves, which it claims to elucidate: the genesis of the world, the material structure of life, the existence of consciousness, and the relation between these and the intelligible world of the true God. There was nothing simple about these problems and even the most reasonable of the Church Fathers often plunged into highly abstruse explanations of them. After all, what we are concerned with here is nothing less than an effort to broach the unknown, to apprehend a world whose laws, structures, and governing forces elude our understanding. And it is not by accident that whenever a problem of this nature is presented to human reason the attempt to clarify it, to unify complex and contradictory given data, is couched in terms which a layman finds difficult to grasp. Let me give another example, still more to the point in that it was revealed to me fortuitously in the course of reading for this book. In *The Universe in the Light of Modern Physics,* a work which appeared a few years ago, Max Planck takes into account the new vision of the world proposed as a result of research done by physicists, and writes the following lines:

'The Quantum Theory postulates that an equation subsists between energy and frequency. If this postulate is to have an unambiguous meaning, that is, a meaning independent of the particular system to which it is referred, then the principle of relativity demands that a momentum vector shall be equivalent to a wave-member vector; in other words, the absolute quantity of the momentum must be equivalent to the reciprocal of the length of a wave whose normal coincides with the direction of momentum.' A theoretical comprehension of this text requires not only a previous initiation into the jargon and given data of the new physics, as will readily be believed, but also and above all else an attitude of mind, the attitude of contemporary physics, in which an innovatory hypothesis demands a total rethinking of earlier systems, and in which the questions addressed to the mystery of the material universe are changed both in character and in meaning.

Without wishing to draw an exact parallel between the studies, the men and the texts, for they can scarcely be said to have plausible links between them, I still believe that one must interpret the innovative vision of the Gnostics in the same fashion, without looking at it only in terms of its structure. To arrive at a consciousness of the nature, the behaviour, and the celestial trajectory of an Aeon, one must have a particular attitude, one which tends to overthrow preceding systems and offers a probability rather than a certainty; moreover, the very word 'Aeon' suggests to the layman that we are talking about some kind of ancestor to the Electron, the Neutron or the great Positron. Paradoxically, it is through a very real need to understand and to explain the nature and destiny of the world we live in in rational terms that the Gnostics, using the hypotheses of their era as a springboard, came to stray into the realm of mythological systems.

I have taken this momentary dip into the world of modern physics only to illustrate how easy it is to sneer at the laboriously constructed systems of the Gnostic masters, which is just what a contemporary layman is inclined to do when faced with any text by those Gnostics of the present day, Einstein, Planck, and Heisenberg.

St Irenaeus, the Christian author, is doing precisely that when he gives us a witty and inspired parody of a text by the Gnostic Valentinus, whose cosmology was peculiarly abstruse: '. . . There exists an intelligible pro-principle, pro-denuded of substance, a prorotundity. In this principle resides a property which I call Cucurbitacy. In this Cucurbitacy is a property which I call Absolutely-void. This Cucurbitacy and this Absolutely-void have emitted without emitting a fruit which is visible in all its parts, edible and tasty: the Marrow. In this Marrow resides a virtue of the same power: the Melon. Cucurbitacy and Absolutely-void, Marrow and Melon have emitted the multitude of Valentinus' hallucinatory melons.'

So, let us pass on to Valentinus and his hallucinatory melons. For this purpose we return to Alexandria. In this city of feverish activity, the Gnostics appear in effect as inactive aliens, preoccupied with Aeons, Filialities, and more or less hallucinatory 'melons.' It is a pity that the Christian authors were too prudish to give us the information which some of them possessed concerning the life and day-to-day conduct of the Gnostics. We have no idea how strong a following a Basilides or a Valentinus was able to command in Alexandrian circles. Certainly they could have had little influence with any but the city's Greek, or Hellenized milieux, for at that period the great Gnostic masters, like Basilides and Valentinus, taught in Greek.

The latter, educated in Alexandria, later went to Rome where he resided for many years. Unlike the other Gnostic teachers, Valentinus began as a Christian and, indeed, narrowly missed entering the priesthood. But his highly unorthodox ideas aroused first distrust and then hostility. Driven out of the Church, he left Rome and journeyed to Cyprus where he founded a community of disciples.

The simple thing to say about his system and his teaching is that, like those of his predecessors, they are very nebulous and exteremely hard to grasp. But one must not overlook the hypothesis that this springs from the failure or inadequacy of the Christian authors to understand what they were writing about. The one certain and immediately discernible fact is that the fundamental themes of Gnostic thought reappear in the *Gospel of Truth* which is attributed to him. In Valentinus' text, the dominant factor in the origin of the world is no longer Illusion but Error, an Error emanating from the unknown and alien Father and in its turn engendering Oblivion, Anguish and Terror in the immense void of the universe in gestation. It is from Them that we originate, we carry Them within us, and that is why Valentinus calls this world, which is the fruit of Error, Oblivion, Anguish, and Terror, the world of Deficiency.

Our feeling of solitude and perdition, the planetary malaise which is man's lot, stems from this original Error that threw imperfect seeds and premature beings into an immature world. We live under the signs of corruption and want. We are lacking in everything: divine oxygen, hyper-cosmic fire and, above all, truth, which has remained in solitary splendour in the upper regions of the hyper-world. We live in the world of death, a death that is both material and cosmic, and of which inert matter is the most tangible sign. And it is only by parcelling it out, scattering it, dissolving it little by little, by consuming all the substance of this world one way or another that man will succeed in wrenching himself free of the circles of Error. 'You must share death amongst you in order to exhaust it and cause its dissolution,' says Valentinus to his disciples, 'so that in you and through you death may die.'

This idea reappears in the beliefs of most of the Gnostic sects, and it justifies the frenzied 'consumption' of matter, in the guise of sperm and desire, indulged in by the most liberated among them. It is in any case the idea which dictates the behaviour of Valentinus' disciples. By consuming the hostile matter of this world—by using up love, flesh, the most sensual and voluptuous pleasures, and by profoundly disordering the human senses (points of junction between matter and life), we will exhaust matter and thus accede to a superior condition which will permit us to rediscover the truth and our lost immortality, to become, in Valentinus' own terms, indestructible beings.

For this world, crucible of corruption, excrement of Error though it is, possesses the seeds of immortality and a faint resemblance to the distant God, the living Aeon, the veracious Model of all things. Valentinus gives us a revealing comparison: 'Inasmuch as the portrait is inferior to the living model, so is this world inferior to the living Aeon.' It is he, this model with the true features of God, whom we must rediscover through the tangled images of this world. Moreover, Valentinus is among those who have traced the different stages of this liberating 'consumption,' working from the Platonic schema. Right at the bottom, in the abyss where the refuse engendered by Error accumulates, is our world of flesh and matter. Men who identify with it all their lives and cannot tear themselves free, who participate in its existence without in any way lightening its matter, will forever remain *hylics,* or material men. For them, there is no salvation. Their destiny is definitive corruption, the ineluctable end of all that is flesh. Above this are the two circles of Air and Ether, composed of matter but lightened and refined, the first step in the climb towards salvation. These circles may be reached by those who have been able to transform matter into psyche by consuming it—that is to say by lightening and filtering it, transmuting it sufficiently to create a soul for themselves. This is the second category of human beings: the *psychics*. But simply to possess a soul is not enough, if this soul is cut off from truth. To perfect oneself, to throw off the ultimate shackles forever, one must know where Truth lies. One must possess gnosis. And here we have the third and certainly the rarest category of human beings: the *spirituals* or *pneumatics,* in other words, the Gnostics. They will gain the highest circle, the circle of the Pneuma or the Spirit.

Perhaps this hierarchy also corresponded to the different stages of initiation reached by Valentinus' disciples. It is difficult to say. One only knows that for Valentinus all three states of man could be identified in the everyday world: the hylics were the pagans, steeped in matter through ignorance of the true religion; the psychics were the Christians who through the grace of Jesus Christ had received a first revelation but were still ignorant of his secret teaching and the profound nature of Truth, accessible only through gnosis. The pneumatics were the Gnostics, who thus placed themselves above the Christians.

One thing is certain—and we know this through the teaching of Ptolemy, who was a follower of Valentinus and author of a *Letter to Flora*—and that is that anyone who had attained the pneumatic state was, in the eyes of the disciples, totally freed from the fetters and corruptions of material nature. To him, all things might be permitted, since his soul had henceforth cut the umbilical cord which tied it to the world of here-below. This is clearly stated in one of Ptolemy's texts, quoted by St Irenaeus: 'Just as it is impossible for the material man (hylic) to be saved, since matter itself cannot be saved, so it is impossible for the pneumatic man to be damned, no matter what his deeds. And just as gold retains its beauty in the depths of the blackest mud and is not sullied by it, so the Gnostic cannot be sullied by anything whatever, nor lose his pneumatic essence, for the events of this world can no longer have any effect on him.'

And here St Irenaeus specifies, in some detail, the nature of the Gnostic's enfranchisement with respect to his material deeds: '. . . The most perfect amongst them also commit forbidden acts without the slightest shame. They do not hesitate to eat the food offered up to idols. They attend all the pagan festivals. Many of them even attend those fights between beast and beast which are abhorrent to man and God alike, and those single combats wherein men fight one another to the death. Others indulge unreservedly in the pleasures of the flesh, declaring that flesh should be rendered unto flesh and spirit unto spirit. Others again secretly despoil the women they seek to initiate. Others, having fallen in love with a married woman, openly and without scruple abduct her and make her their concubine. Finally some of these, who at first pretend to live with her honourably, as with a sister, are unmasked, for the sister becomes pregnant by the works of the brother. And all the while they are committing these bestialities and impieties, they treat us as imbeciles and idiots because we abstain from such acts out of our fear of God. They proclaim themselves to be the perfect ones, the chosen seeds. They pretend to have received a particular grace from on high, as a result of an ineffable union. And this is why, they tell us, they must apply themselves ceaselessly to the mystery of sexual union.'

Thus, in this single example, we see the Gnostics who followed Ptolemy, emulator of Valentinus, consciously and deliberately practising free love, seduction, incest, and all the violations of convention that one could wish for. However, in spite of the acrimony of the witness, and the visible horror these practices inspire in him, something emerges from his accusation: first, the Gnostic's absolute conviction—Luciferian without a shadow of doubt—that he is indestructible, invulnerable to the corruptions of the world; and second, this blatant cult of woman, of sex and Eros, which is the essential part of their lives, the royal road which conquers death and all his undertakings.

VII

ABSOLUTE EXPERIENCE

The most absurd of all earthly laws is
the one that has the temerity to say:
'Thou shalt not covet thy neighbour's
wife,' for it repudiates community and
deliberately chooses separation.

EPIPHANES

In his book on Gnosticism, Leisegang has this to say about the
Alexandrian sects and the general Gnostic attitude to the world:
'... Aversion to love and its consequences, justification of a
counter-nature which they elevate to the level of nature, elimina-
tion of effort, a feeling that only one person in a thousand can
understand them, megalomania, asocial behaviour, traits characteristic of decadence.' On re-reading this sentence, I become aware
of a patently obvious fact which until today had nevertheless totally
escaped me: I myself am a decadent. Apart from megalomania—
for I do not believe I have succumbed to this temptation—I lay
claim to all the attitudes indicated in this text. I do not know
whether they have quite the same meaning and the same implications today as they had formerly, but I cannot help feeling a sense
of familiarity, of solidarity even, with the tendencies quoted above
and all that they imply in life. If decadence really consists in posing
to one's contemporaries the crucial questions that the Gnostics
asked, if it means seeing all systems, laws, and institutions as products of an alienating mechanism, if ultimately it implies an attitude of doubt, rejection, and insubordination towards organized
authority, then long live decadence! For, far from being an outcome of surrender or resignation in the face of the inevitable, it
appears on the contrary as an intellectual lucidity, a searching
inquiry that will leave no stone unturned, and an ambition—arro-

71

gant, no doubt—to question all the philosophical or religious solutions that man has hitherto proposed. In a sense, this radicalism and intransigence, together with the shocking behaviour which was their practical, everyday expression, are at the roots of the failure of Gnosticism. This failure—at least on an historical and institutional level—was written into the very nature of Gnosticism. For the counter-nature the Gnostics preached, the counter-life they attempted to lead on all possible levels, implied in turn a system, or an anti-system, which ran out of steam precisely because of its own refusal to 'exist' and to set itself up as an institution. In attempting to break down existing institutions without proposing any alternative other than a kind of manic outburst of desire, the Gnostics were very soon bound to collide with a fact that is obvious enough (though they undoubtedly failed to foresee it), and that is this: even anti-societies must reinvent their own laws if they hope to endure. The Gnostics, however, caring little for the foundation of lasting schools and having no other aim than to throw off the heavy shackles of this world, accorded no importance to organization and devoted themselves to the ephemeral. This visceral distaste for any attempt to organize and regulate their own revolution, this refusal to guard against the consequences which, in worldly affairs, were inevitable, explains why these sects had such a brief life-span, and why they were suddenly effaced from history like those clouds which suddenly form in a saturated atmosphere, only to vanish again with equal suddenness . . . passing clouds in the mystical sky. Without much risk of error, we may imagine that Alexandria— that city saturated with experience, with gnosis, with messages, schools, and sects—housed swarms of miniscule Gnostic sects, each springing up and disappearing in the course of one generation, each bearing a brief and intense history, an inspired message, and an inevitable death. This is one of the curious but not surprising features of their history: that it endlessly makes itself over anew, like an invisible chain in which, in order that a new link may be born, another must die.

In my view, nothing better exemplifies this inevitability than the bizarre history of the Carpocratians. This sect was active in Alexandria at the same time as Basilides and Valentinus, but unfortunately this does not mean we can say much more about them, for the figures of these Gnostic masters are so vague, so uncertain, so sketchily outlined by contemporary writers—whose primary object was to describe their teaching and not the men themselves—that it is impossible to imagine their features. No doubt, in their outward appearance they resembled the Greek philosophers whose teaching they sometimes adopted. But how exactly did they dress? What did they eat? Where did they live? How did they teach? No author, pagan or Christian, has concerned himself with these matters. We only know through indirect witnesses that they recruited their following from the same milieux as the Christian preachers, and that, in the second century, could only mean the cultured and Hellenized circles of Alexandria. The one certain fact, as far as their schools are concerned, is that women played an important role in them, not only as 'partners,' but as initiates and initiators.

Of the three great Gnostic masters of Alexandria, the most engaging and the most remarkable seems to have been Carpocrates. He was Greek, a native of the island of Cephalonia; his mate was named Alexandria and his son Epiphanes. From his earliest youth, Epiphanes was brought up on Platonic philospohy and the teachings of the Gnostics, and he very soon became a veritable master. His precocity was astounding. He died, in fact, at the age of seventeen, leaving behind him a treatise *On Justice,* which Clement of Alexandria quotes from at some length. His body was taken to his native island, where he was interred with divine honours. These, then, are the only historical images of the sect's founders conjured up for us by their contemporaries: we see an eminently enlightened and well-informed couple, and their son, an adolescent possessing encyclopaedic knowledge and a precocious genius . . . a Gnostic Rimbaud.

If one leaves aside the somewhat singular doctrine they professed regarding metempsychosis and the transmigration of souls, the teaching of the Carpocratians is not particularly different from that of other Gnostics. Nevertheless, the Christian authors tear them apart with a fury for which we must be grateful, since we owe to it our knowledge of certain details of their practices. The point is that the Carpocratians pushed the essential principles of Gnosticism to their logical conclusion—theoretical and practical—and applied, *stricto sensu,* the teaching of Carpocrates and Epiphanes. In their eyes, this world is the work of inferior angels who turned the will and the intentions of the true God entirely to their own advantage. And this 'perversion of intent' had two notable consequences: first, it denaturalized the desire for coïtus, which God had put into man and all living creatures, and made it a slave to the conventions of society; second, it destroyed divine Law by setting up the fragmentary laws of this world. The logical outcome of this teaching is clear: in order to rediscover the pure source of desire and of the true Law, the Carpocratians had to violate the false laws of this vile world everywhere and on all possible occasions. Here, immorality is raised to the status of a rational system, total insubordination is lauded as the road to liberation; a Christian author of the time expressed it in these words: 'According to them, man must perpetrate every possible infamy in order to be saved.'

Yet the most interesting aspect of this subversive thinking is that the Carpocratians seized primarily upon the social forms of this perversion. They had a particular hatred for injustice and its major expression: property. For Epiphanes, divine Law was a law of Justice and Equality. God did not want the good things of this world to be parcelled out among men. Epiphanes demanded the abolition of all property, a return to the absolutely communal possession of goods and chattels, that is to say, of wordly wealth and of women. And here I must quote the admirable text (written when he was only fifteen or sixteen years old) in which he denounces the injustice of this world and the perpetual iniquity of human laws; it is a naïve but impressive vision:

Where does Justice lie? In a community of equalities. A common sky stretches above our heads and covers the entire earth with its immensity, the same night reveals its stars to all without discrimination, the same sun, father of night and begetter of day, shines in the sky for all men equally. It is common to all, rich men and beggars, kings and subjects, wise men and fools, free men and slaves. God made it to pour out its light for all the beings on this earth in order that it would be of common benefit to all: who would dare to appropriate the light of the sun to himself alone? Does he not cause the plants to grow for the common good of all the beasts? Does he not administer his justice equally to all men? He does not make the plants to grow for such and such an ox, but for the whole species of oxen, for such and such a pig, but for all pigs, for such and such a goat, but for all goats. Justice, for the animals, is a benefit they own in common.

And everything that exists, everything that lives, is subject to this law of justice and equality. Nourishment was provided for all living beings without singling out or favouring one species. The same is true of procreation. There is no written law concerning it, for such a law would inevitably be false. The animals procreate, couple and beget according to the laws of community which were inculcated into them by justice. The Father of All gave us eyes to see with, and his only law is that of justice, without distinction between male and female, man and woman, reasoning and unreasoning creature. As for the laws of this world, it is they and they alone which have taught us to act against the law. Individual laws fragment and destroy communion with divine law. The prophet said: 'I had not known sin, but by the law,' and how are we to interpret his meaning, if it be not that the words 'mine' and 'thine' have entered into this world through the laws, and that this made an end of all community? Nevertheless, that which God created, he created for all to hold in common possession: vines, grains and all the fruits of the earth. Has the vine ever been seen to chase away a thief, or a thievish passeriform? But when man forgot that community means equality, and deformed it by his laws, on that day, the thief was born.

In the same way, God created the pleasure of love equally for all mankind and he made the male and the female to couple together and manifest his justice through the community and equality of their pleasures. But men have repudiated the very thing which is the source of their existence, and they say: 'Let he who has taken a wife keep her for himself alone,' whereas all should share in her. . . . God instilled into every man the powerful and impetuous desire to propagate the species, and no law, no custom, would be able to banish this desire from the world, because it was God himself who established it. Moreover the dictum: 'Thou shalt not covet thy neighbour's goods' is absurd. How could this same God who gave man desire wish to take it away from him again? But the most absurd of all earthly laws is the one that has the temerity to say: 'Thou shalt not covet thy neighbour's wife,' for it repudiates community and deliberately chooses separation.

These words have a familiar ring. We have been hearing them and reading them for a long time now. They express an urgent need proclaimed, long before Epiphanes, by Antigone, Epicure, and Diogenes and, after him, by many Utopian thinkers and philosophers. But it is not so much the naïveté and ideological illusion of this thinking—this Rousseauist attitude that all appropriation is robbery and injustice—that matters here, as the practical conclusions drawn from it by Epiphanes' disciples. For without a shadow of doubt they applied these principles, practising a free and common ownership of women and chattels. The awe of the Christian writers, the horror one reads between the lines of their testimonies, suffice to confirm it. No doubt the Carpocratians also opposed all institutions: marriage, family, Church, Authority in all its guises. A total refusal accompanied by sovereign contempt.

For the Carpocratians, the Gnostic's first task was therefore to use up the substance of evil by combatting it with its own weapons, by practising what one might call a homeopathic asceticism. Since we are surrounded and pulverized by evil, let us exhaust it by committing it; let us stoke up the forbidden fires in order to burn them out and reduce them to ashes; let us consummate by consuming (and there is only one step, or three letters, between 'consuming' and 'consummating') the inherent corruption of the material world.

This 'homeopathic' doctrine of salvation explains one of the most curious aspects of Carpocratian teaching: the belief in metempsychosis. If the soul during the course of this life has not succeeded in experiencing everything before death, if there still remain certain forbidden areas it has not penetrated, some part of evil it has yet to consume, then it must live again in another body until 'it has acquitted its duty to all the masters of the cosmos.' This threat— which is virtually a curse—hanging over the future lives of the disciple must certainly have incited him to take the plunge straight away, to 'have done with' these masters of the cosmos in his present life, to 'wipe out' his debts to evil at a single stroke—that is to say, in a single existence. Contrary to what one might be tempted to make of this idea, it is a question of asceticism and not of indulgence in pleasure. Nowhere in their teachings did the Carpocratians suggest that man was evil, only that this world had been perverted by inferior angels; it therefore follows that the disciple must have experienced the same feelings as Epiphanes when confronted with earthly injustice and heavenly justice, and that it must have pained him to commit evil. If free love and communal 'orgies'— a term used by Christian authors — were surely a rather agreeable form of asceticism, and no doubt eagerly pursued, it was not necessarily the same with all other forms of 'consummation,' about which, in any case, we know almost nothing. Did they systematically practise incest, abortion, even infanticide (as did certain other sects of whom we shall have more to say later)? St Irenaeus tells us that one of Carpocrates' disciples, prettily named Marcellina, came to Rome to spread his teaching there 'with painted icons, illuminated with gold, representing Jesus, Pythagoras, Plato and Aristotle.' While it is true that the Gnostics had a propensity for distorting the texts of the Gospels—and even rewriting them when necessary—they could hardly have quoted Jesus as saying: 'Suffer little children to come unto me that I may murder them.' The legends that were rife in pagan circles regarding the 'abominable rites of the Christians,' by which were meant the eating of foetuses and other banquets of this kind, were, in fact, based on a misunderstanding. What seems certain is that in the case of an unwanted pregnancy the Carpocratians did not hesitate to practise abortion. Numerous Gnostic documents are quite clear on this matter. But their teaching, in its very nature, advised against procreation: why bring a creature into the world only to teach him later on that his sole task is to escape from it as swiftly as possible? These 'accidents' must certainly have occurred in the communities that practised communal love. But nowhere in the Carpocratian texts can one

find the slightest encouragement either for procreation or for infanticide.

There is, however, one interesting detail to be found in the
Christian authors' testimonies concerning the Carpocratians; it is
mentioned especially by St Irenaeus and later by Eusebius of
Caesarea. It is the use of drugs and various ingredients during communal orgies and banquets. 'They also practise magic,' St Irenaeus
tells us, 'incantations, love philtres and agapes, the evocation of the
spirits of the dead and the spirits of dreams, as well as other forms
of necromancy for, so they say, they have power over the princes
and over the creators of this world and over all other creatures.
They have, indeed, given free rein to all their aberrations by claim-
ing that they are totally at liberty to perpetrate any act they feel
like, for it is human law (they say) which makes a distinction
between that which is good and that which is evil. Also, by passing
on from one body to another, the human soul must exhaust every
kind of experience. I dare not say or hear or even think what things
have been going on in our cities. But their writings declare it: The
soul must have experienced everything before death.' And St
Irenaeus states a little farther on: 'That done, the soul will no
longer have need of a body. And they add that Jesus taught his
Apostles a secret doctrine and charged them to transmit it to those
who would be capable of understanding it. It is faith and love
which save. All the rest is a matter of indifference.'

One clear fact emerges from these texts: the Carpocratian orgies
were definitely based on ritual. This ritual involved magic, love
potions, and necromancy. Here we are a long way from Basilides
and Valentinus. But on the other hand we are coming closer to
Simon Magus, who used 'sorceries' and accomplished 'many prodigious feats.' Of course, one must remind oneself that the Christian authors—with one exception, of whom we shall speak later—
had access only to indirect evidence, and they could have been mis-
taken as to the meaning and nature of these rites; they could even
have confused the Carpocratians with some other Hermetist, non-
Gnostic group. Nevertheless, the use of philtres—probably aphrodisiacs — is an interesting pointer, for one finds it again in other
sects. Apart from the use of aphrodisiacs, incense, and various
potions or philtres, it does not seem that the Carpocratians made

use of drugs, in the proper meaning of the term. And in any case these magical practices were certainly no more than accessory to the Carpocratian doctrine. What singles it out — over and above the ritual and the teaching itself — is this overt, persistent call to carnal and social insurrection, this absolute contempt for all the laws and conventions of this world, and it is through this attitude that we may discern, struggling to decipher words weighed down with darkness and with time, the figures of these eminent men, and the radiant message of Epiphanes.

VIII

THE ASH AND THE STARS

I am the voice of awakening in the
eternal night.

It is to St Epiphanius that we owe the only first-hand account we
have of a Gnostic community. In his work, *Panarion* or *Remedies
Against the Heresies,* he lists the sects known to him in his own day,
that is to say, in the fourth century: there are sixty of them. This list
is probably not exhaustive but in any case the exact number of
Gnostic sects scattered throughout the Near East from the third
century on is unimportant. The reader will not be surprised by their
number and wide distribution since the reasons for this have
already been shown.

In spite of their multiplicity and the often confusing nature of
their mythology, these sects retain a common feature: they are all
Gnostic, that is to say, they propound the same overall scheme to
explain the genesis and history of the world; one finds the same
archetypes, the same primordial tragedy, the same partition of the
universe into an inferior world of darkness and a superior world of
light. The only distinctions between one cosmology and another
lie in the processes which brought about this alienating separation
and the celestial personages who are involved in it—Aeons,
Archons, Mother, Father, Sophia, Barbelo.

It is not the purpose of this book to make an inventory of these
differences, nor to examine in detail the tangled undergrowth of
Gnostic sects, in the manner of a naturalist of souls. It is my pre-
ferred aim to try to seize upon the common points which distinguish them as a whole from all other religious systems of their time,
and to do this through an examination of the archetypal visions
which are at the roots of Gnosticism and through the rites and

everyday attitudes which proceed from them. For the essential bond between all these groups certainly seems to be this radical rejection of the world, this existential agonizing over man's fate, this urgent need to create a soul for oneself, and the feeling, so typical of the Gnostics, that *everything is given to man at birth, but that he gains nothing thereby.* The rites, practices, and initiations to which they submitted were not gratuitous games designed to fill up their leisure time and justify their theories, but genuinely ascetic exercises, techniques of a vital and singular nature designed to overcome the pitfalls of nothingness and force open the gates of immortality.

Amongst all these sects, there are three which immediately strike one as being very close neighbours: the Ophites, the Sethians, and the Peratae. No doubt specialists in Gnosticism will cavil at my linking them together, but I do so here, and even identify them with one another, because all three offer an almost identical vision of the alienating mechanisms of this world, starting from the same archetypal image: the Serpent.

Moreover, the Ophites take their name from the Greek word *ophis,* meaning snake. For them, the whole history of the world begins and ends with the Serpent. They choose the most unified and the most universal symbol—that of the snake biting its own tail—to represent the destiny of the universe and the continual cycle that goes from the One to the All and comes back from the All to the One. This formula may well appear to be an abstract and arbitrary statement, but, in fact, it is an expression of the most concrete thinking, common to many of the earth's peoples: the coils and writhings of the snake are symbolic of the laws inherent to this world, being at once their sign and their image. Every snake biting its tail becomes a circle, a circle which the Gnostics discover over and over again at all levels: the cosmic level, where it is called Leviathan and its rings encircle the whole of the Hebdomad (the seven planetary circles ranging from the Earth to Saturn), thus constituting the ring that divides the domain of darkness from the domain of light; the terrestrial level where, under the name of Ocean, its complex windings encircle our planet like a gigantic river (and the analogy between water, river, and snake is a familiar one); at the human level, where its coils constitute the intestines, wherein foodstuffs undergo metamorphosis and life is nourished and sustained.

Thus, the snake resides everywhere, at all levels of the created universe, in the body of man, at the extremities of the earth, and at the confines of the sky. He surrounds, separates, protects, and assumes all the life-processes. Naturally, this image is also to be found, in an objectified form, in the Gnostic myths and theories. Where else would one find the snake, if not at the sources (in the literal and in the figurative meaning of the word) of all youth and all knowledge, at the roots (where snakes like to nest) of the trees of Life ? It is precisely because of his two powers: the ability to over-come death (by his successive metamorphoses), and the possession of primordial knowledge regarding the true nature of the world, that the Gnostics see the snake as man's first Initiator and also as the first Rebel in history. In Eden, it is he who sets himself against the authoritarian order of Jehovah, the false God, and reveals to man the secrets of his birth and destiny.

In Gnostic cosmology, this reflection is taken even further. It is interesting to note how the sects mentioned above imagined the means the snake employed to 'liberate' Adam and Eve. He did this, quite simply, by 'seducing' Eve in the Garden of Eden, that is, by penetrating her. But, say the Sethians, the serpent also 'seduced' Adam in the same way. In other words, he deflowered, through the appropriate apertures, both the ancestors of humanity, thus providing them with a double revelation: pleasure and knowledge. For the Gnostics, this act evidently had the force of example and no doubt certain of them did *also* practice sodomy in the name of the serpent, as a ritual repetition of his first act, a way of opening up the 'passages' of knowledge and thereby unsealing the blind eyes of the flesh. One can well imagine how horrified the Christians were at this individual interpretation of Genesis and the Gnostics' practical application of it ! But it is also beyond question that this practice of sodomy, whether by way of exploration, consumption, or consummation of Eros in all his forms, was nothing more than one among many techniques of erotic asceticism: normal coitus, lesbianism and no doubt fellatio (a strict enactment of the image of the snake biting its tail). The term *inversions,* so oddly used by sexologists to designate these heteromorphous erotic practices, would certainly have delighted the Gnostics: was it not their aim, in this domain as in all others, to bring about a total inversion of the values and the relationships between man, his fellow-creatures, and the world?

The Peratae take their name from the Greek *peran,* which means to overcome, to pass beyond. Moreover, they explained themselves in these terms: 'We are the only ones who know the laws of generation and the path by which man entered into this world, therefore we are the only ones who know how to walk this path and overcome corruption.' No doubt the Peratae achieved this 'overcoming' through the same heteromorphous erotic techniques, re-enacting the Serpent's first act which remained the essential symbol of their cosmology and their soteriology: 'Just as a magnet will attract only iron to itself, and amber only scraps of paper, so the Serpent, to the exclusion of all others, attracts from this world only that perfect race formed in the image of the Father, made of the same essence as He Himself is made and which He sent down here below.'

As for the Sethians, who took their name from the third son of Adam, born after the death of Abel (and not of Eve but of the demon Lilith, according to Hermetist traditions), they developed a cosmology very similar to that of the Ophites and the Peratae, but insisted still more strongly on the sexual element. Throughout their texts, the entire history of the world reads like an erotic novel, a cosmic fornication between the original powers and the Aeons of the universe.

If one were to analyse the erotic vision of the Sethians in greater depth, one could say that they especially favoured the feminine sex —largely through the importance they accorded to the eye, which is a reflection of the divine pneuma and the place in which the luminous emulsion of the true God is deposited like a seed from on high—whereas the Ophites and the Peratae, through their exaltation of the snake, favoured the masculine sex. This predominance of the female sex is evident again in the Sethians' image of the world, for the entire universe is visualized as a matrix carrying the virtualities of all creatures in the form of imprints, just as, according to them, one can see the imprints of the life-to-be in the striae which mark the belly of a pregnant woman. They find this image of the pregnant belly reflected yet again in both earth and sky—in the rotundity of the one and the domed shape of the other. To look at the abdomen of a pregnant woman is to see the universe in miniature. Moreover, everything is so closely bound together, so interwoven and imbricated in these revealing analogies, that the woman's labour, the efforts she must make to expel the child, is, according to the sayings of the Sethians, an exact reproduction of the contractions and the obstetric process through which the world itself came into being. They use the image of the sea to evoke this process—swelling, subsiding, heaving, as wave follows wave beneath the fury of the wind, for it was from a wave that man was born, a wave that, impelled by the fecundating wind, by the divine Breath, rose up to the sky, where it received the seed of the Spirit and then, pregnant with all our destinies, fell back upon the shores of this world. Foam, winds, whirlpools, the uterine cries of waves big with the seeds of heaven, a torrential childbirth brought forth in the midst of the cyclones of the Pneuma, the Wind which, once again, is based on the image of the Serpent: '. . . for the impetuous and terrible Wind unleashes its whirlwinds like a winged serpent unwinding its coils. And it was through this wind, through this winged Serpent that creation began. The light and the Pneuma were received into the chaotic womb of the waters and the Serpent, the wind of darkness, the first-born of the waters, penetrated therein and the womb conceived and engendered man.' And so we see repeated everywhere—on land (at the foot of the tree of life), or in the water (close to the shores of the first world)—the reptilian coitus to which we owe our existence.

It does not require much imagination to see that this ophidian cosmology, this vision of the snake as begetter, initiator, and de-flowerer, would have found its expression in the ritual practices of these sects. In fact, St Epiphanius describes an ophidian rite in an account which seems to refer to the Ophites. The ceremony unfolds as follows:

Bread is brought in and piled up on a table in the centre of the hall of initiation. Then a coffer is brought in containing a tame snake. The creature is taken out and put on the loaves while the customary prayers are being recited. The snake uncoils itself, slithers over the bread and the mere fact of this contact, together with the power of the prayers, suffices to consecrate the loaves. They are gathered up and each man or woman present takes communion by kissing the snake on the mouth and then eating a piece of bread. The serpent is therefore credited with the same power as the consecratory words in the Christian liturgy: the power to transform bread into the eucharist.

This simple rite—and all the mythology it implies—is a clear indication of the gulf that already separated the Gnostics from the Christians. For the latter, the snake is, *par excellence,* the utterly damned beast. For the Gnostics, he is the chosen one. Here, then, we see the working of that mechanism, that *inversion of values and symbols,* which was an aspect of the counter-life led by the Gnostics, a mechanism which tended to favour, to invest with power, light, and efficacy all those whom the orthodox tradition looks upon as the damned: Seth, the Serpent, Cain. It is these first Rebels in the history of the world whom the Gnostics were to raise to the highest dignity, to claim as the founders of their sect and the authors of their esoteric books. *Their mythical history thus transmutes itself into a counter-history which places the great rebels in the foreground.* There existed, for example, a sect of Cainites who venerated Cain because he had killed his brother, denied the bond of blood, and thus had become the first to oppose one of the primary alienating laws of this world: the law of the family. It would be wrong to conclude from this, however, that the Cainites preached and practised fratricide. What they undoubtedly venerated in Cain—and, similarly, what the Ophites, the Sethians, and the Peratae venerated in the snake—was an image, a mythical model, an act of rejection whose import was positive for them because it set itself against the order of an evil world *at a time when all things were still possible.* Later, the situation was no longer the same, and the Cainites had no recourse other than a refusal to procreate and found families, a refusal to submit to the alienating order of legally constituted communities. But in each case this refusal has the same purpose: it is an attempt to reconstitute the original unity of the world, to rediscover that time when nothing was yet divided, to regain once more the innocence of Eden. This explains the varied and perplexing nature of the grounds on which each sect chose to do battle against the fragmentation of this world. Some of these grounds were purely symbolic. For instance, in the case of the Adamites, of whom St Augustine tells us that they practised ritual nudity and 'assemble naked, both men and women; naked, they listen to sermons, naked they pray, naked they celebrate the sacraments and say that, because of this, their church is paradise.' Or those Saccophores, that is to say, the wearers of sackcloth, who took against alienating clothes and dressed in sacks or in cast-offs, in anything that would express a rejection of the gulf dividing the rich from the poor.

In this way, each sect chose its own field of action—no matter how humble it might appear—and some of them confined themselves to this partial insubordination. But the most significant battlefield, the most highly-charged in terms of outrage, revolt and liberation, is still the domain of sex. It is the one deliberately chosen by several curious sects whose adherents are called—most improperly—the licentious Gnostics.

In about the year 335 AD, St Epiphanius went to Egypt to study the teachings of the Desert Fathers. He stayed first in Alexandria, and it was there that a unique experience befell him, an experience he deplored, but to which we owe our only eye-witness account of a Gnostic sect. Epiphanius was then twenty years old and, it seems, still naïvely innocent. This explains why he saw not the slightest malice in the proposals of several young and pretty Gnostic women who persuaded him that they alone held the key to his salvation. He followed them, was introduced to members of the sect, became familiar with some of their works which he was given to read, and —probably once only—attended a group ritual. The experience was shattering, and the horrified Epiphanius recovered from it with some difficulty, whereupon he ran to the Bishop of Alexandria to denounce the outrageous scenes he had witnessed. As a result of his action, twenty-four Gnostics were excommunicated. Let us note, incidentally, that this shows the size and importance of this sect. Membership was confined to the 'chosen Vessels,' the 'urns of felicity,' which meant the prettiest Gnostic women, and recruiting must have been highly successful, for this particular sect alone boasted at least a hundred members. Let us also note that these Gnostics called themselves Christians and formed part of the Church up until the day when, through Epiphanius' intervention, they were driven out.

The sect in question was one of those grouped together under the generic name of Barbelognostics. I will give a brief summary of their doctrine since it is essential to an understanding of the scenes that follow.

They took their name from Barbelo, the female power who lived in the eighth heaven (the upper circle of the Ogdoad), whence she commanded the Archons. She herself was the offspring of the unknown Father, the real God. She bore a son called Sabaoth who reigned over the seventh heaven. And it was here that everything went wrong. For, instead of recognizing the authority of his Mother and submitting to the true God, Sabaoth believed himself to be the true God and claimed dominion over all creation. Moreover, he was quite explicit on this point: 'I am,' he said, 'the Eternal One. There is no other God but me.' Faced with this usurpation, Barbelo realized that the fate of the world had gone awry and she must remedy the consequences of her son's insubordination. But how? By seducing the Archons one by one so as to lure them away from Sabaoth's influence. The Barbelognostic text says: 'She showed herself to them in an impressive form, seduced them and collected their sperm with the aim of absorbing back into herself the Power that had become scattered in several different beings.' Such is the first act through which the salvation of the world is inaugurated: Barbelo's power, fragmented in each being in the form of sperm, must be 'recovered,' the primary unity must be reconstituted.

It is not difficult, therefore, to imagine the formula for the Barbelognostic ritual: it is a re-enactment of Barbelo's deed, in other words, a gathering-up of the sperm of each male present. It was this ritual that the horrified Epiphanius attended.

They own their women communally and, in case a stranger should arrive, they have a sign of recognition which is exchanged between the sexes: on shaking hands, each tickles the other's

palm, a sign that the newcomer belongs to their religion. As soon
as they have thus acknowledged one another, they fall to feast-
ing. Exotic dishes are served and everyone—even the poor—par-
takes of meat and drinks wine. When they are completely sated
and, if I may so express it, have filled their veins with a super-
abundance of energy, they fall to debauchery. The man leaves
his place beside his wife, saying to her: 'Get up and perform the
agape (love-union) with our brother.' Then the wretches set to
fornicating, all together, and although I blush at the very idea
of describing their unclean practices, I will not hesitate to dis-
close them, for they themselves have no shame in their perfor-
mance. Once they are coupled together, and as if this crime of
prostitution were not bad enough for them, they offer their
infamy to the heavens: the man and the woman gather the
man's sperm in their hands, raise their eyes to heaven, and with
their hands full of their uncleanness, offer it to the Father, saying: 'We offer you this gift, the body of Christ.' Then they eat
of it and take communion with their own sperm, saying: 'Here is
the body of Christ, here is the Paschal Lamb for which our
bodies suffer, for which they confess the passion of Christ.' They
do exactly the same with the woman's menstruation. They
collect the blood of her impurity and take communion with it in
the same manner, saying, 'Here is the blood of Christ.' But,
whilst they practise these obscenities, they preach that one must
not beget children, for it is purely out of sensuality that they
indulge in these shameful acts. They perform the voluptuous act
and stop just at the point of satisfaction, collecting their sperm
to prevent it from penetrating any farther, and then they eat the
fruit of their shame.

Let us pause for a moment and summarize this ritual in less outraged tones: we note the practice of owning their women in total
community; agapes or orgies during which transient couples make
love indiscriminately (it goes without saying that no sentimental
choice is involved in these acts which are, let us repeat, conceived
of as an ascetic discipline); the practice of *coitus interruptus* to
avoid impregnation and in order to collect the sperm; finally, the
consecration of the sperm which is transsubstantiated into the body

of Christ and the Eucharist, in other words, spermatophagy. Further, let us observe that this ritual is strictly heterosexual and involves no act of sodomy. The latter might, of course, seem to be the simplest means of diverting the sperm from the path of fecundation, but the archetypal model forbids it, indeed, it implies quite the contrary—participation and probably initiative on the part of the female, following Barbelo's example, and from this one can infer the probable custom of fellatio. No doubt Epiphanius turned his shocked eyes away from this act. But let us go on:

> When one of them accidentally allows his sperm to penetrate too far and the woman becomes pregnant, listen to the still more abominable things that they do. They extirpate the embryo as soon as they can take hold of it with their fingers, take this abortion, pound it in a kind of mortar, mix it with honey, pepper and various revolting condiments including perfumed oils, then they assemble together—a veritable herd of swine and curs— and each one takes communion, dipping his fingers into this *paté* of abortion. The 'meal' concluded, they end the ceremony with this prayer: 'We have not allowed the Archon of Voluptuous Pleasure to make fools of us. We have remedied our brother's error.' This, in their eyes, is the perfect Communion. They practise other abominations of all kinds. During their meetings, when they enter into a state of ecstasy, they smear their hands with the filth of their sperm, spread it everywhere and, with their hands thus sullied and their bodies stark naked, they pray that through this action they may obtain free access to the presence of God.

There is apparently no reason to doubt Epiphanius' testimony. If we possessed eye-witness accounts of other sects, they would surely describe scenes that varied only in their minor details. These variations—implicit in the creation-myths which differ from sect to sect—could include sodomy, incest between brother and sister, fellatio and foetophagy. This last 'variation' is mentioned only in connection with the Barbelognostics, but it is most unlikely that they had an exclusive monopoly of the practice, and the rumours —current amongst the Romans—of the secret abominations of

Christian ritual, find their explanation here: they refer only to certain Gnostic sects. Since the latter frequently called themselves Christians, the Romans made no distinctions between true and false devotees of Christ, which accounts for the confusion and misunderstanding.

But, in spite of all this, one cannot give absolute credence to Epiphanius' report. There is something untenable about the scenes he describes—at least in so far as the eating of the foetus is concerned, for the Gnostics were not innovators in any other respect—and one must also remind oneself that the prudishness, naïvete, innocence and inhibitions of many of the Christian authors prevented them from tackling these problems as we can today, by taking them out of their ethical context, stripping them of their emotional connotations, and looking at them as known forms of sexual deviation.

However, the Gnostic deviations are different in kind from those the sexologists study in that they are perfectly conscious and deliberate, and are carried to their uttermost limit as a form of liberating and ascensional asceticism. If they fly in the face of conventional taboos, then it is a problem only for the consciences of others, not for the Gnostics themselves. Of course someone is bound to hurl back the accusation that the myths and delirious fantasies which are pleaded as the authority for these practices are nothing but the sublimated projection of their own cravings, and so one can argue round and round in circles. This is what inevitably happens whenever one is confronted by a deviation or perversion that is consciously justified and deliberately acted out by an individual: how does one find the exact point of departure in this cycle, this game of mirrors in which the unconscious urge and its conscious assertion are reflected back and forth? If we look once more at that very revealing image of the serpent biting its own tail, we can see quite clearly where this crucial point, the site of fusion between the impulse, its mystical translation, and its ritual reflection lies: it is there, where the mouth joins the anus, the point of junction between the fragmentary unconscious and the totalizing conscious mind. I make no claim to justify these singular practices at any level whatever, and I must admit that some of them have only a very limited appeal for me. I have never eaten a foetus and I must say that, until the day when I read Epiphanius' account, the idea had never occurred to me, not even in an oneirocritical form. But it is conceivable that, once the mythological context of these practices was lost and the soteriological system that produced them totally forgotten, they simply degenerated into black magic rituals and Luciferean practices. The Black Mass is not far removed from the Barbelognostic ritual—certainly no farther than Sabaoth is from Lucifer—and it is no mere chance that certain aspects of these rites are to be found, right down to the present day, among the Luciferean sects, where they are spiced with cabbalistic demonology. The ambivalence of the whole Gnostic attitude, the perpetual temptation that oscillates between rigorous asceticism and rigorous debauch (since both have the same soteriological value) is to be found there and, in the historical evolution of Gnosticism, was translated into the opposing paths of mystic Catharism (for the first) and magic Luciferism (for the second).

As I have already noted, the term 'Barbelognostic' designates a number of sects who must have based themselves on more or less the same archetypal systems and practised the same rites. These sects, enumerated by Epiphanius, comprised the Nicolaites, the Phibionites, the Stratiotici, the Levitici, the Borborians, the Coddians, the Zacchaeans, and the Barbelites. I would like to linger over two of these, the Borborians and the Phibionites, whom certain Christian authors considered as identical. The mistrust, horror, and sense of outrage aroused by these sects did not die with them. To this very day, many Christian commentators continue to be struck by the same shudder of horror and repulsion that Epiphanius experienced when he had to speak of them and study them. Let us take, for example, the venerable *Dictionnaire de Théologie Catholique* and open it at the word *Borborians:*

> Gnostics particularized as men of revolting immorality. Tertullian reproaches them for their deplorable obscenity and for other sacrilegious misdeeds. Clement of Alexandria says 'they wallow in voluptuous pleasures like billy-goats and plunge their souls into the mud.' It is the word mud—*borboros*—which

serves to describe these heretics on account of the obscenity of
their customs. Hence their name, which means they are unclean, like mud. Did they really wallow in mud, or is this just
a metaphor?.... They are also called Coddians (from the Syrian
codda: a dish or tray), for none can eat with them. They are
served separately, as unclean creatures, and no one can break
bread with them, on account of their infamous way of life.

One fact stands out immediately: these words do not give any
definition of the sects in question but use invective, contempt, and
insult. But they pose another and more important question regarding the names by which the Gnostic sects were known. Gener-
ally, these names came not so much from the Gnostics themselves as
from their adversaries. It is a phenomenon which still exists today
—we see it in the history of political sects and political heresies.
It is a well-known fact that the terms 'deviationists, revisionists,
class-traitors,' do not define any group as such but simply oppon-
ents whose 'deviationism' may take the most varied forms. Working from this premise, a detailed study of the terms employed by
orthodox Communist parties over the last half-century to describe
heretics of all kinds would throw a most unexpected light on the
history of the first centuries of the Church, for there one finds
exactly the same attitudes. I mention this fact only in order
to point out that a historian, several centuries hence, who set out to
write a history of the Deviationist Group during the first fifty years
of Communism (using only the orthodox political texts) could not
but write a false history, for the very good reason that such a group
never existed. We find ourselves faced with an analogous problem
regarding the Gnostics, as the names they have been given are often
quite arbitrary. Let us take the specific case of the Borborians.
Their name could be a matter of an insulting appellation of purely
Christian origin—meaning the Muddy or Dirty Ones—or a name
that the Gnostics applied to themselves, but in a different sense, of
course, to designate man's first and congenital condition, the *hylic*
condition already referred to in our discussion of the Valentinians.
The word can therefore indicate any human being whatever, or,
in a more limited sense, the condition of a disciple who has joined
a Gnostic group but is not yet an initiate.

This seems still more likely with the Coddians. The isolation mentioned in the *Dictionnaire de Théologie Catholique* is surely not some degrading punishment but a ritual practice. It could refer to the first stage of initiation, a collective retreat on the part of all the candidates, which like all known examples of its kind would involve a temporary withdrawal from the community. In this case, it would be a term used by the Gnostics to designate a particular group, a term which the Christian writers wrongly took to be the name of a separate sect. The names quoted by Epiphanius give several interesting pointers on this subject. Thus, the Stratiotici (meaning Soldiers), the Phibionites (meaning the Humble Ones), and perhaps the Zacchaeans, would be terms referring to different stages of initiation. From what we know of their customs and practices, we can deduce that the two latter states, the Phibionites and Zacchaeans, would be equivalent to the Perfect Ones, the Elect, the ultimate stage of initiation through which the Gnostic gains immortality, indestructibility, and the definitive impossibility of being touched by any defilement.

What we do know for certain is that the Phibionites—whether they were a separately constituted sect or the Perfect Ones within a group bearing another name—had a fashion all their own for proving that they were henceforth invulnerable to any sullying of the flesh. In their cosmology, the circles which separate the earth from the Luminous World number 365. Each of them is governed by an Aeon. To consume the substance of evil, the Phibionite must therefore pay his dues to each Aeon and collect his seed, 365 times during the course of 365 sexual unions with 365 different women. In fact, this is extremely logical; it is only the number of 'consummations' that is startling. But it is dictated by the archetypal myth which, moreover, some commentators believe to be at the origin of the daily Saints' names on our calendar. Be that as it may, here we have the ultimate stage of Gnostic 'licence': the attempt to consume this world of dispersion in which the divine sparks and the Pneuma are fragmented and scattered by consuming the seeds of man and the days of the Aeons, by exhausting and using up, day after day, the maleficent substance of time.

The practices revealed in these lines and in the commentaries they gave rise to in their own day have provoked the greatest anger from Christians. It is because they touch on that forbidden domain of sex, which was always—as Freud amply demonstrated—a Pandora's box which nobody, whether conservative, reformer, or revolutionary, dared to open. Only the Gnostics were bold enough to put a match to the hypothetical gunpowder and postulate that all rebellion, all protest against the world, all claim to spiritual or social liberation must, in order to be effective, begin with a liberation of sex. I do not think I need repeat here a point which I have already stressed several times: namely, that the Gnostics do not necessarily translate this attitude into a frenetic debauch and the daily consumption of sperm. Many Gnostics, beginning with the greatest, Basilides and Valentinus, adhered to asceticism pure and simple, but it was a matter of total indifference to them whether or not their disciples followed this path.

One consequence of this attitude which was particularly innovatory in its day was the importance accorded to women in these salvatory asceticisms. In the rites, the cults, and the mythological speculations, woman played a major role, as the receptacle of light and as an initiator. The terms by which the Gnostics called her: chosen vessel, urn of felicity, not only placed her on an equal footing with the male but recognized her as the possessor of a favoured particle of the original Power. One must not make the mistake of deducing from the Gnostic orgies that woman is treated as an object here, an instrument of pleasure, as was to be the case later on in the works of the Marquis de Sade and in contemporary debauches, where erotism is reduced to the level of a sensual pleasure without myth or salvation. We are confronting one of the rare examples in history where woman appears invested with a regenerative power and a salvatory mission. But she was there by virtue of her sex and not as an individual. Each was a fragment of original Woman—of Sophia or Barbelo—and during the course of these orgies each man coupled not with a woman but with Woman. The difference is crucial, and if the Gnostics were able to magnify sex and at the same time reject love as a sentiment, if they achieved a total and radical dissociation between these two domains, it was because all the force of their love, their sense of fusion and indentification, was turned towards the true God, the distant kingdom which they could reach only with the help of woman, through her and with her.

And so we see that in the very depths of corporeal darkness, in the world of ash and mud that is each human body, only an all-embracing asceticism or only the effusion of erotic desire and the ecstatic cult of woman can revive the flickering spark we keep within us. Just as the ash at the heart of a dying fire glows red, being the burned-out stars of matter which has been consumed and, by the same token, ultimately saved, so, for the Gnostic, the mental embers that glow red in the ashes of the body, when liberated and saved through gnosis, are the sure sign that his path will one day lead him to the circle of the stars.

IX

THE IMPOSSIBLE MIRROR

> When Jesus descended into Hell, the
> sinners listened to his words and were
> all saved. But the saints, believing as
> usual that they were being put to the
> test, rejected his words and were all
> damned.
>
> MARCION
> *Antitheses*

The deviations and inversions, the spermatic and magic rites, the mythologies and hallucinations which are attributes of the Gnostic sects of Alexandria must not mislead us into overlooking a fundamental fact: studied only in terms of the rites which were their practical expression, these Gnostic attitudes seem aberrant, naïve, and even perverse. But as soon as one turns one's attention to the masters, the teachers and sages of Gnosticism, one encounters men of great culture and erudition, men who scrutinized the universe, the world, and their contemporaries with exceptional lucidity and penetration. In spite of their relentless intolerance of the Gnostic sects and their 'shameful' practices, Christian authors could not but recognize the human worthiness and the spiritual radiance of men such as Basilides, Valentinus, Carpocrates, and many others. Such are the contradictions and, at the same time, the riches of Gnosticism: while it satisfies all the demands of the intellect through the lucidity and radicality of its outlook, it sometimes dampens the ardour of sympathizers because the application of its theories has such strange results in daily life. One cannot with impunity play with the fire of heaven or the divine spark of the psyche, and many Gnostics must have burned themselves at the braziers they had deliberately set ablaze. In attempting to delve deeply into the aggressive and destructive impulses of desire, and to liberate

96

and thereby exhaust them, they often played sorcerors' apprentices of the soul, and did so at a time when the realm of the unconscious was as yet unknown. It is indisputable, however, that they had a presentiment of the existence of this realm and clamoured loudly for man's right to burn himself in his own delirious fire. In the entire history of Western thought—although Gnosticism is also of oriental origin and does not wholly belong to our world—I know of no attempt that aimed so high and was so charged with lightning flashes of insight and seeds of intuition, no endeavour that was so fruitful in producing positive revelations. And this is why I say again that one cannot write a history of Gnosticism as one would write a history of the Knights Templar, the Camisards or the Reformation. As this book progresses, as page follows page, I become increasingly aware that Gnosticism is insidiously affecting me and drawing my whole being into the questions that I put to it. In all that I have written so far, where does my personal interpretation of Gnosticism begin, where does it end? It constantly brings me back to myself, for, throughout a history which it denied, a future destiny which it fought against, Gnosticism never ceased to ask itself, and to ask those who enquired into it: Who are you? Who am I to take up this shadowy history of rejections and secrets, to retrace these deliberately concealed paths, to try to pierce these Hermetic revelations whose very Hermetism exasperates me but which, I am totally convinced, are not gratuitous?

My conviction goes still further: I believe that these paths show us the only possible way, the only way of acting in the face of the mysteries of the world. One must try everything, experience everything, unveil everything, in order to strip man down to his naked condition; to 'defrock' him of his organic, psychic, social, and historic trappings; to decondition him entirely so that he may regain what is called by some his choice, by others his destiny. As I write this word, *decondition,* I perceive that I am reaching the very heart of Gnostic doctrine. No knowledge, no serious contemplation, no valid choice is possible until man has shaken himself free of everything that effects his conditioning, at every level of his existence. And these techniques which so scandalize the uninitiated, whether they be licentious or ascetic, this consumption and consummation of organic and psychic fires—sperm and desire—

these violations of all the rules and social conventions exist for one single, solitary purpose : to be the brutal and radical means of stripping man of his mental and bodily habits, awakening in him his sleeping being and shaking off the alienating torpor of the soul.

For my part, I find it strange that all the books written about Gnosticism leave their authors untouched, as if it were a matter of writing a chapter about some interesting but slightly cracked and utterly depraved historical people. Moreover, the questions posed by the Gnostics remain posed for all time, yet I cannot see that those who studied them ever realized that these questions were addressed to them, too.

I am well aware that one never writes a book that is not about oneself, and, if the problem of the Gnostics has long interested and preoccupied me, it can only be because it concerns me at a level of which I myself am unaware, and of which this work can give only a superficial—and more or less consciously veiled—analysis. Why am I particularly attached to those who are known as the licentious Gnostics, since historically, numerically, and philosophically speaking, they represent only one sect among others ? Am I the unwitting victim of a phenomenon born in my own time, one which leads us to interrogate ourselves more deeply than ever before on sexual questions ? Is my need to give it preference due to the fact that I am not sufficiently deconditioned ? Or does this Gnostic revolt against sexual taboos express a preoccupation which is fundamental to all periods of history, because it is truly at the roots of all liberation, but which they alone expressed, without reticence and without inhibition ?

At this stage, I find it difficult to make up my mind. However, one aspect of this book, its options and orientations is quite deliberate and conscious: it is not meant to be a history of Gnosticism, but rather a meditation, an attempt to define all that remains alive, tangible, and significant in the Gnostic movement, and still concerns us today. I confess to a feeling that I am tackling problems that are difficult to pin down, and chasing shadowy figures who might well challenge the portrait I have tried to draw of them. This is not a ploy to justify the inadequacies of this book. It is simply that I believe it is presumptuous—and even anti-Gnostic—to violate silence and force it to speak, and to reinstate in history (with all its inevitable ambiguity), those who spent their whole lives vilifying it and running away from it.

There is one aspect of Gnostic teaching that has barely been mentioned so far, although it concerns it closely, and that is dualism. Dualism can be understood as any vision of the universe which divides it into two opposing, coeternal, and independent entities: Light and Darkness, Spirit and Flesh, Good and Evil, etc. Defined in this way, dualism appears in many ancient religions and philosophies as well as in certain Gnostic doctrines. For Simon Magus, for instance, there certainly existed two different worlds, two irreconcilable Gods. But this vision, which one finds in its clearest and most fully-developed form among the Manicheans, was not systematically adopted by all Gnostics. For many of them—including some of those we have already discussed—the world of evil did not appear as an autonomous entity, coeternal and coexistent with that of good, but rather as a creation issuing from the hyperworld, arising through error or imitation. Incidentally, it is this distinction which explains the morality or non-morality of the Gnostics: born of a misunderstanding, of a fall or a split, this failed world still preserves something of the substance of the true world, and it is on this that the Gnostic relies when taking on the monumental task of purifying the maleficent substance. In a world where Evil was coexistent and coeternal with Good, one cannot see how man could 'reascend the slope,' cross the abyss—which, in this case, would be uncrossable—and rediscover the essence that is his salvation. Therefore, dualism in the strict sense is not always to be found in Gnosticism, but rather duality, a duality that is based on the genesis, not the essence, of the universe. But it must be pointed out that this duality evolved over the course of centuries and was expressed in forms that came closer to true dualism by Gnostics such as the Bogomils of Bosnia and the Cathars of Languedoc. It was also expressed by a Gnostic of whom I have not yet spoken, who lived some time after Simon Magus and whose work—somewhat singular and marginal to the history of Gnosticism—is worth noting. His name was Marcion.

With Marcion, Gnosticism rediscovers what it was in its very beginnings: an effort of the rational mind, an attempt to reach a logical understanding and, in the light of the Gospels, to rethink the problem of the world's existence and the destiny of man. But this thinking led him to such radical and unforeseen conclusions that, like others of his kind, he found himself excommunicated and driven out of the Church.

Marcion was a native of Sinop, in Pontus, on the northern shores of Anatolia, where he was born in 85 AD. He belongs, therefore, to the same generation as the disciples of Simon Magus. His father was the Bishop of Sinop and Marcion was brought up entirely in the Christian teaching. He acquired such a profound knowledge of the Bible and the Gospels that St Jerome describes him as a 'veritable sage.' But his ideas on Christianity must have appeared very unorthodox for his own father banned him from his community. So Marcion chartered a boat and, like St Paul, launched himself upon the waters, there to preach his doctrine. Several years later, we find him in Rome, where he settles down, frequents the Christian community and, for many a long year, shrouds himself in silence in order to set down his ideas in writing. The fruit of this labour is the publication, starting in 140 AD, of those *Antitheses* in which he expounds his theory of the world, his interpretation of the Bible and the Gospels, and the principles which, in his view, should govern the founding of a new Church.

I can do no more than summarize these principles here, but I must immediately underline one outstanding fact: contrary to all other Gnostics, Marcion wanted above all to establish a Church, to found secure and settled communities whose Gospel would be his *Antitheses.* This in itself was sufficient to get him barred from the Church, but he continued to teach, and with considerable success it seems, for he had thousands of disciples. Tertullian says that 'they fill the whole universe' to such an extent that, for some time, they constituted a real threat to the official Church. Three centuries later, Marcionist churches are still to be found in Rome, Cyprus, Egypt, Palestine, and Syria.

For Marcion, the basic problem is eminently simple. A reading of the Old and New Testaments (it is to Marcion himself that we owe these terms, which are common currency today) shows two universes, two incompatible orders. The Gospels reveal a God of love and goodness, whose Son has come down to earth for the express purpose of saving men and teaching them fraternity, mercy and love for their neighbours. The Old Testament, on the other hand, shows a God of justice and chastisement who persecutes humanity and always appears surrounded by thunder and lightning. He knows nothing of generosity, clemency, or tolerance. The history of the world and of man, as they appear in the Bible, are made up of crimes, massacres, and blood. They manifest a world which is intrinsically evil and corrupt, a universe that is indisputably a failure, and a mankind that has miscarried. Something is sadly amiss with this creation that Jehovah is constantly forced to punish, and wherein man lives under the permanent threat of taboos, fulminations, and terrorization by the Creator. Therefore, says Marcion, it is impossible that Jesus, who is the Son of God, should be the Son of Jehovah the exterminator, or that the latter could be the Father whom Jesus claims. Marcion arrives at the same logical conclusion as Simon Magus: Jehovah is not the true God. The latter is the Unknown God, a stranger to this world, the true Father whose Son is Jesus Christ.

The merit of Marcion's system—in comparison with Simon Magus's—is that it is infinitely more rational and its exposition is based on a scrupulous interpretation and a minutely-detailed philological knowledge of Biblical and evangelic documents. He does not need to enliven this doctrine and this vision of the world by calling upon prodigies, sorceries, and all the magic paraphernalia with which Simon larded his teaching. The implication of Marcion's ideas is thus seen to be simple but revolutionary: the Bible is not and could not be a work of revelation, nor a Holy Scripture. The opposition between the Old Testament and the New is total and it is expressed at all levels: in the genesis of the universe and in the texts which narrate this event. What the Bible describes is not the immense and grandiose work of God, but the stultifying creation of Evil.

It would be pointless to pursue in detail all the evidence which Marcion amasses, through quotations from the Pentateuch, to support his *Antitheses*. What is significant is the specific inference Marcion draws from them: faced with the evidence of two worlds and two messages, it is clear that only the Gospels convey the teach-

ings of the true God. The Old Testament must be relegated to everlasting oblivion.

All the same, the message of the Gospels has not survived intact,
it is not entirely free of additions, interpolations, 'revisions' of all
sorts introduced by the Judaists and the earliest disciples of Jesus.
In order to be certain of attaining the truly divine word, Marcion
purifies the Gospels and sifts through the distortions to which they
have been submitted to find the authentic text, the only canonical
work, which will serve as a foundation for his entire doctrine. This
text, beginning with the Gospel according to St Luke, is the one he
proposes in his *Antitheses.*

Without wishing to draw too many implausible and in any case
debatable parallels, I would suggest that, in its day, this original
and revolutionary attempt must have had the same impact that, in
our day, the publication of some socialist *Thesis or Antithesis,* re-
pudiating the Marxist doctrine and relying exclusively on a
corrected edition of Lenin's speeches, would have. I know that this
notion is absurd and inadmissible since Lenin himself constantly
quoted Marx as his authority. But what interests Marcion is not
solely the textual message of Jesus—which must be reclaimed from
the dense fog of distortions to which it has already been subjected
—but also the necessary work of adaptation that he himself must
do so as to render it effective and vital in a world which is not, and
has not been for a long time, the Biblical world of nomadic shep-
herds. Today, we can see clearly that the problem is not so far
removed from the one faced by Socialist intepreters of Marxism;
and when the most recent and authoritative commentators on
Marx speak of 'a rereading of Marx,' and write essays entitled
Rereading Marx, they are using almost word for word the same
terms as Marcion himself, whose teaching could in fact be summed
up in the formula: *Rereading the Bible.* This was why his endeavour was so innovatory, the reason he was judged a heretic and condemned to silence or, at the very least, to retirement: that he sought
to snatch adolescent Christianity from its Biblical shell, to break
with a dogmatic tradition which was believed to be indispensable
to its evolution; to open up new paths; to rethink and re-evaluate
the schemata proposed by the Bible and decide whether they were
valid or null and void. In so doing, he claimed to re-orient Christ-

ianity and the new man whom he called into being towards the future, a future still to be fashioned, improvised, built up day by day on the basis of the Gospels alone and thus to destroy forever the image of the false God.

It is impossible to imagine how the history of the Church might have developed had it adopted Marcion's theses. Obviously, its evolution would have been utterly different, and from the second century on, it would have taken up certain positions which, eighteen centuries later, it is slowly beginning to make its own. However, incapable of wrenching itself free of a tradition and a mythology which furnished it with both an ethical framework for its message and the emotional visions without which it would have had nothing but abstract principles, the Church was forced for centuries to drag in its wake images, geneses, and apocalypses which in fact were alien to it. Marcion came too early into a world that was not yet ready to accept the liberating rupture, to undergo the 'harrowing revision' which would have broken the mooring-ropes that tied it to the Bible. Nevertheless, this far-sighted and courageous effort did not completely die out with Marcion. The longing for an adult Christianity, boldly confronting the problems of its time, liberated from the everlasting references to Genesis and the Mosaic commandments, is not altogether dead. But it is not easy to tear oneself free of the mirages, of the factious and factitious mirror of the Bible, wherein man has never ceased to read his own false image and to follow his false destiny, and wherein the Church for such a long time managed to lose its way and wander like Alice in Wonderland.

The Paths of Gnosticism

> Against whom shall we do battle, where shall we direct our attack, when the very breath in our lungs is impregnated with the same injustice that haunts our thinking and holds the stars in stupefaction?
>
> EMILE CIORAN
> *A Short History of Decay*

X

THE WORLD'S WANDERERS

They spend their time doing nothing
and sleeping.

TIMOTHY
On the Messalians

From the fourth century onward, the history of Gnosticism changes
its locale, its nature, and its meaning. It is no longer written in the
cities but, as in its beginnings, all along the highroads of the Orient.
After leaving Egypt and dispersing throughout Mesopotamia,
Armenia, Cappodocia, Greece, Bulgaria, and later Bosnia, Gnosticism takes on very different forms from those which we have seen
hitherto. It is as if, by a sort of cyclical return to their earliest aspirations, the Gnostics flee the cities to take up their wanderings once
more along the roads, on the plains, and in the mountains. With
only a few rare exceptions, it is there that we shall henceforth discover the new Gnostic communities—communities whose way of
life, principles, and techniques (ascetic or licentious) retain their
autonomy and their strangeness, and whose excesses and insubordination will once again bring down upon their heads the thunder-
bolts and excommunications of the Christians. Simultaneous with
this return to the earlier wandering life, this nomadic existence
without hearth or home, this rejection of towns and all permanent
settlements, is another significant fact: the doctrine itself loses its
coherence, or at the very least its systematic character, the mythology becomes etiolated and the written Gnostic works rarer.
Nevertheless, these groups were numerous and active and I would
like to dwell on one of them, the most spectacular, known as the
Messalian sect.

Their real name — by which I mean the name they called themselves—was the Euchites, meaning the Praying Men ('Messalians'

is the Syrian translation). Their beliefs recall the fundamental Gnostic themes regarding a lower world of darkness and a higher world of light, but they are orientated in a somewhat unusual direction, calling upon mystical effusion rather than the demands of reason.

For the Euchites this world was the devil's handiwork, and everything—matter, flesh, the human soul—was impregnated with diabolical substance. So much so that the devil was physically and psychically present in each man, bound consubstantially to his soul. Similarly, the history of the world—that perpetual struggle between darkness and light—was re-enacted in the history of each individual. It is, therefore, the task of every human being to eradicate the demon that lives parasitically within him, and to do this by special and particular 'shock techniques.' Since from birth every man finds himself thrown into a world which is subjected to the violence of the devil, he must liberate himself through a campaign of equal violence, a ruthless combat against the devil. Seen in this perspective, it is self-evident that neither asceticism nor licence would be sufficient to overcome so powerful and cunning an adversary. Those techniques are double-edged weapons; they are, among other things, cumbrously slow and uncertain. The daily erosion, the grinding down of evil and sin as preached by the Gnostics of Egypt—and which in the case of the Phibionites required at least 365 successive sexual unions—appears to the Euchites outdated and inefficient. For them, the only sure and immediately effective weapon is prayer. But not the traditional Christian prayer. The Euchites practised perpetual prayer, an outpouring of the spirit every moment of the day which plunged them into a second state, opened their souls to the influx of the Holy Spirit, and liberated them forever from the devil. Thus through the medium of incantatory prayer a physical and spiritual battle was waged against the intruding demon, who was eventually expelled by what amounted to exorcism. For this purpose the Euchites chose the Lord's Prayer, which they recited ceaselessly to the point of vertigo and even unconsciousness, stimulating themselves by dancing and by imbibing various concoctions. In this way they attained a state of ecstasy, and possibly convulsion, during the course of which the 'ablation' of the devil took place. This is why they were also known as the Enthusiasts (a word whose etymological meaning is: possessed by God) or the Dancers.

This is the dominant trait of the Euchites, but other interesting aspects of their lives are known as well. Totally preoccupied with carrying on this merciless struggle against the devil, they took little heed of the contingencies of daily life. They refused all forms of work, whether manual or intellectual (which led to their sometimes being called the Lazy Men) and subsisted solely by begging. Men and women lived together in itinerant tribes who wandered along the roads at random (notably in the province of Osrhoëne, around Edessa), slept in the open air and practised communal ownership of women and chattels. They also rejected all obedience and submission to authority—whether ecclesiastical or temporal—which made them not only vagabonds and beggars but outlaws, too. What made it so difficult to constrain and convert them, or even to render them harmless, was the fact that, once they had driven out the demon, they considered themselves, like the Pneumatics, untouched by any defilement and invulnerable to the compromises of this satanic world. Everything became a matter of indifference to them and one can detect a certain embarrassment, and a no less certain irritation, on the part of the Christian authors when writing of these libertarians of Gnosticism who accepted and performed no matter what act of contrition and would admit to anything that was asked of them. In the seventh century, the Christian Bishop Timothy published a work on the heresies of his time; he writes of the Euchites as follows: 'In summertime, when night falls, they lie down to sleep in the open air, men and women together in total promiscuity, and they say that this is a matter of no consequence. They can indulge themselves with the most delectable foods and lead the most voluptuous or the most debauched lives for, according to them, none of this matters in the slightest.' But what shocks the good bishop most of all is the deliberately rebellious attitude of these vagabonds, their insolent refusal to work and their evident propensity for doing nothing: 'They know how to eat of the best without ever having to work for it. And they eat whenever they feel hungry, drink when they are thirsty, at any hour of the day, without regard to the prescribed fasts, and they spend their time doing nothing and sleeping.'

The existence and behaviour of these sects, whose numerical importance in certain regions of the Orient was considerable from the fifth century on (let us say, some tens of thousands of the faithful), created a problem for the temporal powers responsible for maintaining law and order. And they were not the only ones—on many occasions the ecclesiastical authorities tried to disperse these groups or force them to return to the bosom of the Church. But, in order to thwart all these efforts, the Euchites had perfected certain techniques which totally disconcerted their Christian interrogators. They did not hesitate to follow the advice which Basilides had long ago given to the Gnostics of Alexandria, that is: to abjure meekly whatever they were asked to abjure, to submit to baptism, take communion, make the act of contrition and, once they were allowed to go free after this proof of submission, to return immediately to their nomadic life and their habitual practices. Timothy never ceased to bemoan this attitude, whose real motives he did not grasp and which he saw only as the most arrant hypocrisy (which explains why the Euchites were also known as the Liars). St Epiphanius, who devotes a few lines to them while confessing himself defeated in advance by their strange conduct, declares that it was their habit to reply 'Yes' systematically to all questions put to them. And he quotes a revealing example of Messalian response:

'Are you patriarchs?' 'Yes.'
'Are you prophets?' 'Yes.'
'Are you angels?' 'Yes.'
'Are you Jesus Christ?' 'Yes.'

No interrogation, no excommunication could make sense under these conditions. Let them be excommunicated, let them be forced to take communion, the result was all the same. But since the bishops, in their perverse obstinacy, were determined to formulate an act of accusation against them at all costs, one with precise and justifiable charges, they themselves were driven to use lies and hypocrisy to achieve their ends. For example, Timothy reports that the Bishop of Edessa, on an occasion when three of these villains had been hauled up before him, pretended that he wanted to become a convert to their religion. The three Euchites (evidently not so cunning as the Christians had alleged) fell into the trap and revealed their beliefs: man is possessed by the devil and nothing—

neither baptism nor communion nor the sacraments of the Church
—can deliver him from the fiend. Only prayer, perpetual prayer
can cause the Holy Spirit to enter into him and rid him of his
demon. Now, for once, the Church had knowledge of the exact pro-
positions which she hastened to condemn. The three rascals were
excommunicated and returned to their life on the open road.

In this history, one point remains obscure and it seems to me an
interesting one: what was the exact nature of these prayers, these
exorcizing dances which delivered the Euchite from his demon?
Obviously the dances must have called for music. In this respect it
is worth noting that another and more ancient heresy, Montanism,
had been prevalent in the neighbouring regions two centuries
earlier. It was a mixture of Messianism, predictions as to the
imminent end of the world, and practices of an ecstatic character
which were designed to procure for the disciple an immediate
vision of the Paraclete. Now this heresy developed in Phrygia, a
region known since antiquity for its frenetic, effusive music. The
Phrygian mode, played on wind instruments, was used for orgiastic
dances, Dionysian cults, and the mysteries of Cybele. It is possible
that the Euchites used analogous instruments and musical modes
which, in addition to the drinks consumed before the prayers, provoked trances and collective possession. As to the style of their
dance, Theodoret of Cyrrhus speaks of it, in passing, thus: 'they
had ridiculous dances consisting of jumping into the air, while they
made puerile boasts that they were jumping over demons.' The
whole thing came to an end 'in horrible bacchanales in which men
and women mingled.'

Another of their beliefs, pointed out in one of the acts of accusation which, to their very great harm, were set up against them,
seems to me still more significant. The expulsion of the demon and
the presence of the Holy Ghost permitted the Euchite to accede
instantly to the world of light. The splendours of the Pleroma were
unveiled before him and 'they claim,' says the Act, 'to see God with
the eyes of the body.' This was a dangerous affirmation which in
other times would have led the seer straight to the stake. For by
entering into the state of ecstasy, of indifference, of *apatheia,* to use

the hallowed term (that is to say, of impassivity with regard to all worldly concerns), and by acceeding to hyper-consciousness, the Euchites crossed—or claimed that they had crossed—the forbidden frontier which all theologies have drawn between the intelligible (or divine) and the manifest (or human). Evagrius Ponticus, an Anchorite in the deserts of Egypt, says: 'Do not aspire to see either the Angels or the Powers or Christ with the eyes of the body, on pain of falling into madness.' The Euchites, it seems, crossed the great divide. Nothing else in their disorderly, vagabond lives, neither their refusal to submit to any social constraint nor their ecstatic dances, had the sacrilegious force of this simple phrase. More than anything else, it cast them out of the Christian —indeed, out of the human—world.

XI

THE PURITY OF THE MOUNTAINS

.They denounce wealth, they have a
horror of the Tsar, they ridicule their
superiors, condemn the nobles and for-
bid all slaves to obey their masters.

COSMAS THE PRIEST
Against the Bogomils

In the mountains and forests of Bosnia and on the plateaux of
Herzegovina—and sometimes lost in the wilderness—are thousands of sculptured tombs and dozens of necropoli that have posed
an enigma to history and archaeology for the past two centuries.
Their number, their arrangement, their sculptures, the inscriptions
on certain of them attest to the existence of important communities
with a hierarchy and precise customs, whose history is still very
largely unknown. The regions where they predominate indicate
that they were peasant communities, grouped around several fiefs,
at the heart of secluded areas which long escaped the jurisdiction
of the Orthodox and Catholic Churches of Serbia. The mystery
appeared to be solved when these curious constructions were attributed to the Bogomil heretics. The Bogomils, whose name means
the Loved Ones or the Friends of God, were a Gnostic-like sect, the
heirs to neo-Manichean traditions which emerged in Bulgaria from
the ninth century onward. The sect split into several groups, one of
which took root in Bosnia and in Herzegovina, in the heart of
present-day Yugoslavia, over a period of several centuries. These
villages, castle-fortresses, and whole provinces acquired by the
Bogomils are a far cry from the miniscule Alexandrian groups.
Gnosticism enters history, implants itself in the bosom of national
communities, founds its own churches with priests and deacons and
becomes a veritable temporal power in itself. By the time of the

113

Paulicians, another Gnostic sect contemporary with the Messalians, Gnosticism had already ceased to be a clandestine doctrine taught in secret or in the solitude of the desert; as a hotbed of revolt against all the temporal powers, Gnosticism inevitably found itself confronted with the movement of history, and the repressive measures to which it was subjected compelled it to forge a social and political body, an autonomy, a destiny all its own. Wherever it sets foot, wherever the word is spread, it creates pockets of rebellion —religious or political—against the official Church and the secular authority which is its expression. One therefore finds the new Gnostics rising up by turns against Byzantium, the Slav invaders of the Balkans, the Orthodox noblemen of Serbia. Gnosticism now recruits its devotees from essentially rural areas. Moreover, the peasants will be more sensitive to its political and social implications than its religious ones. But, through this bias, the Gnostic groups become virtually communities of insurgents, gathering together thousands of peasants and artisans, and obliged henceforth to establish their own laws, their own organization, and even their own army. Clearly there is something paradoxical about this destiny. Born out of a radical rejection of history and society, Gnosticism by its very success gives birth in its turn to a history and to societies, ephemeral no doubt but whose very existence and tragic fate will nevertheless long remain exemplary.

If the Bosnian tombs and necropoli are indeed of Bogomil origin, then they show the extent to which Gnosticism has changed its face and its history although its doctrine in itself always remains the same. For the first time, one finds oneself in the presence of historically and geographically stable communities, and also of carved monuments, material vestiges—in short, a Gnostic art. On its own, this simple fact would tend to make one doubt whether these sculptured tombs and ornamental monuments could really be the work of groups professing Gnosticism, for nothing up until this point has been more alien to the Gnostic mentality than a concern to leave material traces, especially works of art, behind them. Art, like history, nourishes time and presupposes its existence. It is inevitably written into a time-span which the Gnostic rejects. It is not so much the absurdity or the futility of aesthetic feeling which is in question here as that of its expression. If one could imagine men such as Basilides, Valentinus and Carpocrates showing a concern for matters of this nature (an unthinkable supposition in my opinion), they would have created nothing but a purely symbolic art, didactic perhaps and, in any case, outside of time. But the art of the Bosnian tombs and necropoli is specifically an expression of the rites, games and combats, the daily or religious life of the communities concerned. It is the deliberate reflection, affirmed and repeated everywhere, of the principal moments of their earthly life. What does one see on these tombs? Scenes of rural and feudal life—women dancing, men engaged in chivalrous combats or archery contests, people standing either with both arms raised or the right hand only, fingers spread, deliberately enlarged, in the posture of swearing an oath, perhaps, and around and above them the same cosmic symbols: the sun and the moon.

Some years ago, I visited the sites where the most important of these tombs are to be found, at Radimjle, Cicevac, Hodovo and Boljuni. Most of them are covered in moss and lichen which is gradually effacing and eroding the carved scenes. Rain has gnawed into the stone and sometimes it is only by tracing the outline with the finger that one can recognize a form, a human figure, an animal running, a crumbling planet, the curve of a bow on this granite which, little by little, is returning to its original blankness. An atmosphere of intense mystery emanates from these hundreds of monoliths lost in the forests or on the deserted plateaux, but also one of fear and insecurity in the face of death. These inscriptions aimed at protecting the deceased from profanation of his tomb, these symbols which accompany him everywhere like guardians keeping vigil over his soul, are bearers of an ambiguous message made up of certainty and apprehension, wherein the very gestures of the dead man, his rigid and ritual posture attempt, perhaps, to conjure up the mysteries of the invisible world. Nothing of all this appears to be truly Gnostic and I am doubtful to this day about the religious adherence of these thousands of dead souls. What is certain is that these necropoli are the only vestiges of a society which must have been long-lived and intense: nothing remains of the villages and castles where so many beings, now forgotten, must once have lived. Not the smallest ruin, the faintest trace in these mountains where trees and grasses have covered over the soil and often uprooted the monuments themselves.

Be that as it may, one thing at least emerges from this: the fact that, henceforth, the war against Gnosticism has also changed. Excommunication and imprisonment are no longer enough. Religious and political rebellion by these organized communities entails measures of repression, on the part of the powers-that-be, which will consist of purely and simply annihilating all those who refuse to submit, burning their churches, setting fire to their villages, razing their fortresses to the ground and setting up stakes where the Bogomils, by the hundreds, will throw themselves into the flames. What was it about this heresy that provoked such ruthlessness, such repression? It preached the stand we have long known: a total refusal to compromise with a damned world contaminated by evil and the devil. But this refusal, in the context of this particular epoch, turned principally against the official Churches, against their flaunted wealth and their abhorrent symbols. The Bogomils detested the cross because Christ had died on it and it became, in their eyes, the symbol of his torment. They rejected the whole of the Old Testament, the essential dogma, the Virgin, and all the Christian mythology. They practised a stern asceticism—henceforth no more debauchery or licence, for the historical struggle implies another and equally pitiless struggle, against the temptations of the body. They rejected procreation and marriage; they despised work, riches, honours, social distinctions. Among themselves, each considered all others as his equals. One single distinction—an important one, however—marked their relationships. Since Bogomilism developed above all in a rural milieu where it was vital to work, to cultivate the soil, and to make clothes to ensure the survival of the communities, the rule provided for two states, two separate functions: the Perfect Ones led a totally Gnostic life, that is to say they lived as ascetic mendicants, taught in the provinces, initiated novices, and administered the sacraments. The others, the Auditors or Disciples, constituted the masses who were permitted to marry, procreate, work, and thus ensure the material survival of the group. But this two-fold revolt against the Church and the Authorities—the rejection of the cross, the dogma and the Orthodox sacraments, as well as the refusal to obey the secular powers—soon drew a reaction from the authorities. Now we see thousands of soldiers and Christian priests invading these provinces and indulging to their hearts' content in pillage and plunder, burning everything and massacring everybody in their path. All this bloodshed testifies not only to the odious intransigence of the Church and its Orthodox rulers, but also to that of the Bogomils who, faithful to their oaths and their convictions, refuse to abjure, preferring to hurl themselves into the flames. And it is this suicidal course which will henceforth follow Gnosticism whereever it goes. Faced with the shame of compromise, of submission to the Church and to the army of Satan, Gnostics will uphold the sovereign purity of their own faith, and proclaim it even on the threshold of death.

This attitude will win a halo for the heretics, one that their martyrs will wear for a long time to come. Henceforth nothing but war, the stake, and genocide will succeed in quelling the rebels of God. And even then Gnosticism will not be entirely vanquished. It will be reborn elsewhere, further afield, in the silence and solitude of other mountains, in the heart of the Pyrenees and of the Corbières, where its history will repeat itself, with the same cycle of grandeur and tragedy, up until the funeral pyre of Montségur.

Towards a New Gnosticism

Most contemporary philosophers postulate
the existence of a sentient and more or less
conscious *Anima Mundi* to which all things
belong; I myself have dreamed of the deaf
cogitations of stones. . . . And yet, the only
known facts seem to indicate that suffering
and consequently joy and, by the same
token, good and what we call evil, justice
and that which, to us, is injustice and, finally,
in one form or another, the understanding
necessary to distinguish between these opposites, exist solely in the world of blood and
possibly that of sap. . . . All the rest, by which
I mean the mineral kingdom and the realm
of spirits, if it exists, is perhaps passive and
insentient, beyond our pleasures and our
pains, or this side of them. It is possible that
our tribulations are nothing but an infinitesi-
mal exception in the universal pattern and
this could explain the indifference of that
immutable substance we piously call God.

MARGUERITE YOURCENAR
The Abyss

We have nothing to learn from evil. The world in which the Gnostics lived, whether Alexandrian, Slav, or Provençal, was everywhere and at all times a world of injustice, violence, massacre, slavery, poverty, famine, and horrors patiently borne or savagely resisted. And the Gnostics spoke truly when they said that to experience misery, to let oneself be eaten away by this corrosive rust, is a futile experience. It needs — or needed — all the barefaced hypocrisy of Christian morality to convince the robbed, starved, and exploited masses that their trials were a blessing and would open the gates of a better world to them.

It will be clear to the reader that the word *evil* is used here in a sense which is outside any ethical or religious context. Evil is simply all that which contributes to the world's entropy. And obviously this evil cannot open any gates nor enrich or awaken any part of man whatsoever since it is, in its very essence, that which alienates all consciousness, that which consolidates the false order of the universe.

Pseudo-knowledge, believed to be gained through suffering, the fallacious redemption gained through ordeal, is nothing then but a lie, a lie that fails to recognize—or pretends not to recognize—the absurd and alienating nature of evil. Gnostic soteriology is quite explicit on this point: evil is never at any moment the outcome of a divine plan; it is not a natural or inherent necessity but the product of an error or misunderstanding. It is a material cancer which has grafted itself on to the ethereal particles of the hyper-world, a spiritual chancre which we must extirpate from our psyche instead of nurturing it on the pretext that it will bring about our redemption.

But the nature of the Gnostics' struggle against evil obviously sprang from the times in which they lived. Their mode of speculation and the specific feeling that here and now, during this life, they

121

must forge a soul capable of escaping from the visceral and cosmic corrosion, meant that they took up arms above all on the spiritual plane. It was in man's very consciousness, at the thinking source of his being that they confronted the enemy. And they did this by trying to achieve gnosis, a true awareness of themselves, of man's place in the universe and of his role in its destiny.

The Gnostic paths which we have traced briefly in these pages are not the only ones. I would even say that, in a sense, they all led into a blind alley. The war that the Christian Church waged against the Gnostics' attitudes from the very beginning compelled them, little by little, to do battle on the Christians' own terrain by establishing counter-Churches or, if you prefer, heretical movements which limited the field of action and thought to the purely religious domain. Since its earliest origins, with men such as Valentinus, Carpocrates and Basilides, Gnosticism had sought above all a non-religious or an a-religious attitude, for it was anxious to bypass the absurd antinomy of faith versus knowledge, the sacred versus the profane. They knew that the sacred, like the profane, is vitiated by evil and that the solution could not consist in opposing the first to the second, but in overcoming both one and the other and liberating oneself from the false dilemmas into which they drive us.

This position clearly implied a total questioning of the very existence of the sacred, and therefore of the usefulness of religions and, *a fortiori,* of Churches. This tended to throw the most rational of the Gnostics into a solitary position where few came to join them, but which prefigured the attitudes of certain thinkers, philosophers, writers, and mystics of our own time.

I would define this position as a return to the fundamental, virginal interrogation of man faced with the problems of his life, with his need to escape from the yoke of systems and to arrive, in every instance, at a point of absolute zero in knowledge. If the Gnostics proposed a dualistic image of the world, it was not because, when faced with an entity, they were temperamentally predisposed to see its opposite, but because, confronted with the agonizing and omnipresent evidence of evil, it was necessary to oppose something to it. But their aim was quite patently to overcome this antinomy which did nothing but reflect the schism, the inherent rending in two of the world. By doing this—we cannot say it too often—they found themselves obliged to reject practically all the religious ideologies of their time and to live on the fringes of all accepted conventions, since, for them, the demands of truth were paramount, even if they were to lead them to the stake.

When one undertakes such a purging and uprooting of the human consciousness, when one snatches away from man the mythological and ideological illusions which justify his choices and, more often, his fantasies, it is perfectly obvious that one is exposing oneself, first of all, to every kind of misunderstanding and, still more surely, to every kind of retaliation. Idols cannot be cast down with impunity, and we can see quite clearly where the task of a contemporary Gnostic would lie: in attacking the new idols, the new Churches of our time, in short, the new faces which evil is forever putting on and which today we call ideology.

Ideology has merely set up new graven images in place of the old. For example, in Marxism (one of the dominant idols of our time) one can see an analogous phenomenon, on the scale of the history of men and ideas, to that which the Gnostics denounced on a universal scale: the misapplication, the deflection of a thought—that of Marx—which revolutionary and mutant in itself and its time, has often ended up in fact as a caricature of a society, a mutilated Socialism. Very briefly, one can define this ideology according to the three terms proposed by Marx—to understand, to control, to change the world. Each of these terms is imperatively tied to the preceding one. In order to change the world, one must be able to control its mechanisms, and one cannot control them without first understanding them. It is the last of these three terms that has very rapidly been taken up as the most potent rallying cry, for it is the one that is most highly charged with irrational content. It is, in fact, the only one which appears on Marx's tomb: 'The philosophers have only interpreted the world in various ways. The point, however, is to change it.'

What is most striking in almost all political and social experiments undertaken up to now is that they have effectively changed certain of the material conditions of existence while forgetting, somewhere along the way, *why* they had to be changed. Who remembers that Marx wrote, somewhere near the end of *Das Kapital:* 'Socialism must not become the end but the means through which we change the world we live in'?

However, this is not the sphere that I would choose to define the possible attitude of a Gnostic confronted by the modern world. I have taken it as an example because the birth and progressive triumph of Socialism offer us precise evidence of a phenomenon analogous to that which the Gnostics experienced with the historical victory of Christianity. But just as the latter did nothing but reinforce the power of the Priest—a return to the pagan systems which, in other respects, it sought to abolish—so Socialism has reinforced the power of that latter-day priest of our time, the Policeman. Whatever name he is given, according to the political system in force, he remains the great victor in all revolutions, the one who survives all upheavals. No revolution — except for very brief periods such as the first three years of the French Revolution or the first five years of the Russian—has led to man's achieving an increased libertarian awareness any more than it has ever asked itself what is the meaning and nature of the major cause of alienation: work and the productive effort, regarding which the same general outlook has been preached—and very often in the selfsame words—by all the existing systems. To keep our questioning on Gnostic lines, we may therefore ask ourselves: why must we, at all costs, produce *more and more* goods every day?

I do not want to appear naïve here and suggest that the solution to the problem lies in a total refusal to produce (any more than a refusal to procreate is a realistic solution to the problems of the birth-rate). There will always be a handful of men—some rational, others Illumined—who will preach such a refusal and live on the borderline of the laws and conventions of their time, under whatever regime that may be. But one is well aware that, on one hand, production cannot go on expanding indefinitely and, on the other, that the mode of this production (or, in other words, the relation between the worker and his work) is just as vital and as central to a society as its quantitative results. By way of illustration, I will ask but a single question: why has no Western Socialist system abolished the practice of working on an assembly-line, or at least tried to reduce it substantially? Why preserve (and in some cases even augment) this most alienating of all methods of production, as if the mere fact of nationalizing the means of production and suppressing monopolies sufficed to transform it suddenly into a means of liberation? It will be argued that this problem is so complex and would involve such profound reorganization of the techniques of production that it cannot be envisaged except on the time-scale of a whole generation. Very well, but it should still be done. And it is not being done anywhere, least of all in the places where the power is supposed to be in the hands of the workers.

I do not believe that a rejection of the world in its modern form, a return to communal life, abandoning factory production in favour of cottage crafts and industries, has a future in the world we live in. Not because it is a rejection of the principle of efficiency (the only real efficiency being that which gives meaning to our lives), nor even because it cuts itself off from the solidarity which, in our general misery, is necessary (it is always better to fight alongside the workers than without them), but above all because its motivations are more unconscious and irrational than truly critical. Moreover, this attitude is almost always accompanied by a return or a correlative recourse to religious doctrines, to the teachings of Oriental philosophers, to Zen, to Tantrism, to Sufism, and soon it will be the turn of Gnosticism (the last teaching still to await its adepts and its Enlightened Ones).

A retreat from the world has no meaning unless it implies remaining, in fact, in the world while belonging to it at another level; it must not mean abdicating in face of its complexity or its malevolence, but elucidating its innate laws. This is why the path of absolute withdrawal chosen by a man such as René Guénon, author of *The Crisis of the Modern World* (London: Luzac, 1962; Totowa, N.J.: Rowman & Littlefield, 1962), *The Reign of Quantity* (Harmondsworth and New York: Penguin, 1972) and *Symbolism of the Cross* (London: Luzac, 1958; Totowa, N.J.: Rowman & Littlefield, 1958)—who became a convert to Islam and left France to live and die in Egypt under the name of Abdel Wahed Yahia—seems to me sterile in this day and age. First because it involves a step which is essentially solitary and, second and more important, because his constant search for an original Tradition meant dedicating himself exclusively to a cult of the past.

Gnosticism, on the other hand, has always denied to the past, as to the future, any didactic value. No *total* light can come from an earlier religion or tradition. The tendency to delve into an immemorial past or to project the knowledge-that-will-save into a Messianic future can only distract man from his true quest: the quest for a new consciousness, *springing from his immediate experience and contingent on the present.* It is no mere chance that the only work by René Guénon which I find fruitful—*The Crisis of the Modern World*—dates from 1927, and was conceived and edited at a time when he himself still belonged to his own epoch. The book contains a violent and exhaustive indictment of the contemporary world. But Guénon's aristocratism, his exclusive attachment to esoterism, his arbitrary rejection—and at times, indeed, his faulty knowledge—of contemporary philosophies, plus his ferocious intellectualism prevent his being a true creator.

Moreover, his attitude and his radical choices pose a fundamental question which is linked to our preoccupations here: in postulating a primordial and sacred Tradition, Guénon proposes as a source of contemplation and knowledge the teachings of men who lived centuries ago, indeed thousands of years ago, in a context totally different from our own. But can such teaching really help us? Is it relevant today? All the masters, schools, and sacred texts to which the traditionalists refer lived or were conceived in a world separated from our own by a major difference: it was a world not yet expropriated by man. The earth's matter, animate and inanimate, remained neutral and available, as it were.

But the matter of the modern world lost its virginity some two hundred years ago. The components of the universe — atoms, the chromosomes in our cells, the elements of the natural environment —are henceforth submitted to the actions of man, in a fashion which, for the moment, remains limited and anarchic but which one can well see has transformed evolution into revolution. Now this primordial fact does not lead only to a progressive modification of the material or organic supports of our own evolution, it also modifies, and in a radical manner, *the conditions and the nature of knowledge.* This last, too, must undergo an identical revolution which renders Tradition, if not out-of-date, then at least very relative. The Tradition cannot reply to all the questions posed by the modern world for the sole and simple reason that it was born into a different world, one which never even suspected such a revolution.

I think, then, that true knowledge cannot be sought in the past but only in the future. It is not in any way a question of rediscovering, but of discovering. It resides in that intense and virgin future, whose shape depends far more upon ourselves than Guénon believed. Guénon remains well this side of the Gnostic positions, for he appears to believe that the given data, the structures of knowledge exist—or existed—whereas they have yet to be invented.

Among contemporary writers whose sensibility, modes of thought and references to men and experiences of other ages seem to me very close to those of the Gnostics, I would cite, before all others, Emile Cioran and Marguerite Yourcenar. *A Short History of Decay* (New York: Viking Press, 1975), *The Temptation to Exist* (New York: Quadrangle, 1970) and *The New Gods* (New York: Quadrangle, 1974) by Emile Cioran are texts which match the loftiest flashes of Gnostic thought. I have quoted a few lines from these works as an epitaph to certain chapters in this book, but I would need to quote many more to do them justice. *A Short History of Decay* has, since its publication, been a constant bedside book for me. It dissects our decadence more exactly and incisively than the shrewdest political analyses of the period, in prose nobler and more brilliant than many of the surrealist texts to which it might invite comparison. The radical nature of the questions the author sets before the world—and he makes his presence felt on every page—makes the book both disturbing and trenchant; indeed, it appears to me to be one of the most illuminating of our time, providing, of course, that one can harden one's heart to bear the apocalypses and abysses, the depths of nothingness and non-being which he opens before our eyes. But, then again, its lucidity, its intransigence perforate this existential night with a light as dense and as permanent as that of the stars.

L'Oeuvre au noir (*The Abyss*, New York: Farrar, Straus and Giroux, 1976) by Marguerite Yourcenar is also illuminated by a Gnostic light on every one of its pages. The voice of Zeno, her principal character, even when he expresses himself in veiled words (for sixteenth-century Bruges is not identical with second-century Alexandria), reveals again the forgotten accents and gestures of the

Gnostics. All that the passing of the centuries has given rise to in the meantime—the need to interrogate the very mechanisms of life, to dissect bodies and explore consciousness—in no way deflects Zeno from the path of his Alexandrian predecessors. Simon Magus had already pondered on the role of blood. Epiphanes had discovered in the sun the radiant source of our life and the secrets of justice. In the entrails of man, the Peratae had rediscovered the serpent coiled at the roots of heaven. Like them, Zeno brings a reconciling eye to bear on our world, together with the same demand for sternness, the same courage in face of a possible nothingness. Like them, he will know how to 'enter into death with his eyes open.'

One could find many other examples, more readable from our point of view because they are to be found in a context which is our own. I am thinking in particular of *L'homme imaginant* by Henri Laborit, where once again the problem of the change in our mental structures *through knowledge* is posed in clear terms. Through these examples one sees that all Gnostic paths pass through a double itinerary: the existentialist certainty (let us say, even, the instinctive certainty) of our own incompleteness and the necessity—in order to save ourselves from it or at least attenuate it —of setting out on the road to knowledge. This knowledge implies the biological determinisms, psychic impulses, and economic constraints which govern and manipulate us, in addition to a total participation in the problems and miseries of one's own time. The Gnostic of today could no longer be a preacher of salvation, a holy man living a solitary existence on his mountain-top, nor some illuminated spirit living in a great city and devoting himself to his beloved ancient texts, but rather a perceptive man, his eyes turned towards the present and the future in the intuitive conviction that he possesses above all *within himself* the keys to this future, a conviction he must hold steadfastly against all the reassuring mythologies, the so-called salvatory religions and disalienating ideologies which serve only to hinder his presence in the true reality. For the important thing today is not so much to discover new stars as to break down the new frontiers that constantly arise before us, or which are delineated within ourselves, so that we may cross over them, as into death, with our eyes wide open.

BIBLIOGRAPHICAL NOTES

In the course of this essay, I have deliberately avoided expatiating upon the texts and quotations used in its composition. I will therefore complete this study by adding here a detailed note on the textual sources of Gnosticism and on the works of reference I have consulted.

Our knowledge of Gnosticism and its history rests on two kinds of document: the actual Gnostic texts, that it to say, the surviving works that are considered to be of Gnostic origin, and secondly, the quotations and commentaries found in the Church Fathers' studies of the heresies.

GNOSTIC TEXTS

Up until 1945, authentic Gnostic texts were very limited in number. The best known, the *Pistis Sophia* (Faith and Knowledge), was discovered in Egypt in the eighteenth century. It was written in the Coptic language and first appeared in a German translation in 1851. In 1896, in Egypt, a codex was discovered which contained several Gnostic writings: the *Gospel of Mary*, the *Apocryphon* or *Secret Teaching of John* and the *Sophia of Jesus Christ*. To this, one may add an important fragment of a text entitled *The Book of Ieû*, two prayers and a fragment relating to the soul's journey through the circles of the Archons. This last collection was published in Leipzig in 1905. [An English translation, by G. R. Mead, is available: *Pistis Sophia: A Gnostic Miscellany*, Blauvelt, N.Y.: Multimedia Publishing, 1973.]

Of all these texts, the *Pistis Sophia* is by far the most complete and the most important. I would like to give a brief account of its content, for, aside from the minutely detailed and wearisome descriptions of the multiple circles of the Pleroma, it contains passages of very great beauty. The whole work comprises four books narrating the fall of Sophia (the Aeon whose avatars we have related in 'The Workings of the World'), her lamentations, her redemption through the intervention of the Saviour, that is to say Christ, and the astonishing journey through the splendours of the upper heavens which Jesus accomplishes after his ascension. On his return to earth, He relates the details of this ascension to His disciples and, in the course of dialogues and interviews lasting twelve years, reveals to them the secrets of the universe.

The Ascension of Christ takes place before the terrified eyes of the disciples and is accompanied by a cosmic upheaval that shakes heaven and earth. Jesus rises through the different circles of heaven and reaches the heart of the Pleroma. He reappears to His disciples in a light so dazzling that they cannot look at Him, then He takes on His human form once more and replies to all their questions. A veritable cosmology is thus unfolded, a gigantic fresco describing the totality of the worlds. From it one can learn the whole history and genesis of the universe, the nature and role of the Aeons, each in his own circle, the why and the wherefore of each and every thing. In this work, therefore, we see yet again—in spite of its obviously mythological structure—that need for rational comprehension which was one of the essential aspects of Gnosticism. The existence of evil, of injustice, of all kinds of violence, the why and the how of the light and the darkness, day and night, riches and poverty, the existence of the different animal species, different plants, all this is explained, commented upon, rehearsed. It is, then, one of the fundamental texts of Gnosticism, even though its precise origin has never been determined. Tradition attributes it to Valentinus, but H. Leisegang, in his book *La gnose,* sees it more as the work of a sect akin to the Ophites or the Barbelognostics.

In 1945, some peasants discovered a large earthenware jar in a cliff near Nag-Hammadi, Upper Egypt; it contained a great many Coptic scripts. Jean Doresse, historian, archaeologist and specialist in Coptic Egypt, made an inventory of them, classified them, studied them and drew up the first balance-sheet of this discovery. It was, indeed, a particularly lucky find, for these texts unquestionably constituted the complete library used by a Gnostic sect of Upper Egypt in about the fifth century. Regarding these texts, I shall use the nomenclature adopted by Jean Doresse in his book (of which more below).

The collection consists of fifty-one treatises which Doresse divided into three groups: writings of entirely Gnostic origin, apocrypha of Christian origin and treatises of a Hermetic nature. Here is the list of authentically Gnostic works:

Paraphrase of Seth; Allogenes Supreme; The Secret Book of John (Gospel of John); Epistle of the Blessed Eugnostus; The Sophia of Jesus; The Hypostasis of the Archons; The Book of the Great Invisible Spirit or Gospel of the Egyptians; The Apocalypse of Zostrian; The Apocalypse of Messos; The Revelation of Adam to his son Seth.

THE CHRISTIAN AUTHORS

From the very beginnings of Gnosticism, with Simon Magus, the Christian authors never ceased to pursue it, study it and, above all, refute it, right up to the last moment of its Near Eastern history. This work of refutation concerned not only Gnosticism but all the heresies of the time. However, the radical nature of the questions posed by the Gnostics compelled the Church Fathers to define their own theological position minutely and thus to formulate for Christianity its first fundamental dogmas. The list of these authors is therefore considerable, but since many of them copied or took their inspiration from one another, I will mention here only those who provided the most complete information or carried out the most searching studies.

The most ancient is St Justin Martyr, who published his *Apologies* between 150 and 160 AD in Rome, as well as a work entitled *Against Marcion,* which has since been lost. We have extracts from this, however, in the works of St Irenaeus, who is next on our list; he came from Lyons and it was in that city that he wrote his *Revelation and Refutation of False Gnosis,* better known by its abridged Latin title *Adversus haereses,* in about 180 AD. Then St Hippolytus of Rome, who published the ten books of his *Philosophumena,* or *Refutation of All Heresies* in about 230 AD, and St Epiphanius of Cyprus, who wrote his *Panarion,* or *Remedies*

Against the Heresies, in about 375 AD. Further interesting quotations are to be found in other authors, notably the Church historians such as Eusebius of Caesarea, Theodoret, Bishop of Cyrrhus, and Timothy, who were writing at a later date, between the fifth and seventh centuries. Taken in their entirety, these works furnish very substantial information about the Gnostics, their works, their systems, and sometimes their rites. Some of them, such as St Hippolytus, St Irenaeus and St Epiphanius even quote important extracts from Gnostic writings. It seems they were in possession of a certain number of documents, but one must emphasize that, with the exception of St Epiphanius, none of them had any direct experience of Gnosticism. The works they quoted in order to refute Gnosticism must have been those which were given to new followers, not the secret books which were presented only to fully-fledged initiates. Nevertheless, the information they provide enables us to add a certain number of titles to the preceding list of works written by Gnostics.

For example, a work entitled the *Revelation of a Voice and of a Name* was attributed to Simon Magus, and he himself had this to say of it: 'This writing comes from the Great Power, the Infinite Power. That is why it will be sealed, hidden, veiled and deposited in the dwelling where the Root of All Things has its beginnings.' Basilides appears to have written twenty-four books or *Exegetics* on the Gospels and composed his own gospel, the *Odes,* destined to be recited or sung during the liturgies he had instituted. Valentinus composed the *Gospel of Truth,* which was unknown, except through quotations in the works of the Church Fathers, until 1945, when a copy was found in the Gnostic library of Nag-Hammadi. Today, it is part of the collection in the Jung Institute in Zurich. A translation was published in 1956. Let us add the treatise *On Justice,* by Epiphanes, son of Carpocrates, whom we have mentioned in 'Absolute Experience'.

These were the works of the principal Gnostic masters. But the innumerable sects in Egypt and Syria drew upon a very large number of works, attributed to venerable authors such as Seth (son of Adam), Jesus Christ, the Virgin Mary, or the Invisible Spirit, all of which contained their secret teachings or revelations. A fabulous history was apparently accorded to all these books, such as this one ascribed to the *Sacred Book of the Great Invisible Spirit,* used by the Sethian sect: 'This is the book written by the great Seth. He deposited it in the highest mountains, where the sun never rises. Since the days of the prophets, the apostles and the preachers, his name has not resounded in men's hearts. Their ears have never heard it. The great Seth took one hundred and thirty years to write this book. He deposited it in the mountain called Charax in order that, in due time and in the last moments, it would become manifest.'

Finally, other works, like *The Rulers of the Cities up to the Ether,* must be manuals of initiation, inspired by magic, designed to show the disciple how, after his death, he can traverse the different circles by pronouncing the name of each Aeon or guardian in turn. Here again, one finds an eschatology reminiscent of that of Ancient Egypt, and the themes of the *Book of the Dead* and the *Book of Am-Douat.* It is to be noted that this tendency towards a soteriology of magical character becomes more marked as Gnosticism evolves, and that certain treatises enumerated the innumerable and mysterious names of the guardian entities of the intermediary circles. It is a strange litany—mixing up Barbelo, Sophia and Sabaoth (whom we have already met) with beings such as Prunicos, Harmozel, Eleleth, Ialdabaoth, Astaphaeus, Aberamenthus, Agrammakarei (which means literally: the Indescribable Vault), Anthropos, Athoth, and Adamas. . . . *The Book of Ieû,* a Gnostic text discovered in the nineteenth century, even tells us the magic formula one must not fail to pronounce if one wishes to gain direct access to the heart of the Pleroma. Here it is, commit it well to memory:

> aaa ooo zezophazazzzaïeozaza eee iii zaieozoakoe
> ooo uuu thoezaozaez eee zzeezaozakozakeude
> tuxuaalethukh.

BIBLIOGRAPHY OF GNOSTICISM

Gnosticism, considered as a heresy, forms part of the history of Christianity. It eludes this history, of course, because of its content, its implications and its philosophical or esoteric overtones, but in practice those who took an interest in it were almost all historians of Christianity. The majority, obviously, show no mercy to the Gnostics. After an interval of eighteen centuries, it is easy to laugh at their hallucinatory mythology and to veil one's face from their erotic rites. Rare indeed are those who, denying themselves the easy path of hasty judgements and religious or theological *a priori,* sought to grasp the profound meaning of the questions posed by the Gnostics. Rarer still are those who, on approaching their subject, accepted the necessary deconditioning and the notion that these questions are equally addressed to them, equally relevant in spite of the gap of centuries. Amongst the latter is Henri-Charles Puech, author of several works on the Gnostics and the Manicheans. His two essential texts on Gnosticism are: *La gnose et le temps* (Zurich: Eranos Jahrbuch, Vol. XX, 1952) and the resumé of the course he gave at the Collège de France, published in the Almanac of that establishment for the years 1953 to 1957. These lectures are due to appear in their entirety in two volumes under the title *Phénoménologie de la gnose.* The title clearly indicates Puech's angle of approach to the study of Gnosticism, and it is the only one which seems to me fertile in this day and age. His lectures represent the most sensitive and the most pertinent approach to Gnostic achievements and attitudes we have yet seen.

In the field of textual knowledge and the history of Gnosticism, the most complete and detailed work, the richest in information of all kinds—and the most up-to-date—is the book published by Jean Doresse under the title *The Secret Books of the Egyptian Gnostics* (London: Hollis & Carter, 1960; New York: AMS Press, 1960, reprinted 1972). It consists of two volumes, the first containing a detailed exposé of all the Gnostic systems, such as they were known up until the discovery at Nag-Hammadi, and the second, subtitled *The Gospel according to Thomas,* a detailed account of this discovery, an inventory of the manuscripts found and a translation of the above-named *Gospel according to Thomas.* It was from the first volume of this collection that I borrowed the translation of St Irenaeus' humorous piece on Valentinus and his 'hallucinatory melons', quoted in the chapter 'The Masters of Gnosis'.

I must also mention Serge Hutin's essay *Les gnostiques* published in the '*Que sais-je?*' series. In this work, the author goes beyond a general outline of Gnosticism: with great skill and clarity, he introduces us into the labyrinth of Gnostic thought, following it right down to the present day through its various esoterical, philosophical, and literary aspects. One of the book's most original contributions is that it examines Gnosticism not only as a thing in itself, but also in relation to our own times.

Among the other works, many are available today only in libraries. Most of the historical research into Gnosticism over the past half-century has been done in Germany, and the number of studies is impressive. I will mention here only those which are available in English or in French translation, such as *La gnose* by H. Leisegang (Paris: Payot, 1951, is the latest edition), most ably and sensitively translated by Jean Gouillard (who is also the presenter and translator of the *Petite Philocalie de la Prière du Coeur*, a book which, although not directly concerned with Gnosticism, is an aid to an understanding of many of its aspects). Leisegang's book tackles Gnosticism primarily from a philosophical and theological point of view. It is relatively old (first edition in 1924), but it presents detailed insights into the different Gnostic systems, debatable no doubt but extremely erudite. Finally, a recent work offers new and original perceptions as to the origins of Gnosticism and its links with Christianity. This is *Gnosticism and Early Christianity* by Robert M. Grant (New York: Columbia University Press, 2nd ed. 1966). The same author has also compiled *Gnosticism: An Anthology* (London: Collins, 1961), which consists of a collection of almost all the Gnostic texts known to us today, and is indispensable.

Of course there are other works which, directly or indirectly, are concerned with Gnosticism. The majority of these broach the subject from a partial or specific angle—some of which are crucial, nevertheless, such as the problem of dualism or the relationship between Gnosticsm and Manichaeism. I could not mention them all here, but I will single out those which have been useful to me or which are essential reading for anyone interested in the influence of Gnosticism. First of all, the essay by Simone Pétrement: *Le dualisme chez Platon, les gnostiques et les manichéens* (P.U.F., 1947), Steven Runciman's work: *Medieval Manichee* (Cambridge and

New York: Cambridge University Press, 1947), which deals especially with the Messalians, the Paulicians, the Bogomils and the Cathars, and the 'bible' of this genre, *Love in the Western World* by Denis de Rougemont (New York: Harper & Row, 1974).

It goes without saying that the last part of this book, 'Towards a New Gnosticism', involves no bibliography. In any case, the term is inappropriate, for here it would no longer be a question of a bibliography but of a guide-book to several essential books of our time, and the universes they envisage and reveal, since the eclecticisms, analogies and parallelisms they propound are all entirely personal. They have no other aim than to define the point—omnipresent and impossible to grasp—where antinomies, contradictions, and opposites cease to be such, the point at which several contemporary Gnostics find themselves today — sometimes, without even realizing it.

Printed in the USA
CPSIA information can be obtained
at www.ICGtesting.com
JSHW082214140824
68134JS00014B/612

9 780872 862432